RESEARCH HIGHLIGHTS IN SOCIAL WORK 45

Social Work and
Evidence-Based Practice

Research Highlights in Social Work

This topical series examines areas of particular interest to those in social and community work and related fields. Each book draws together different aspects of the subject, highlighting relevant research and drawing out implications for policy and practice. The project is under the editorial direction of Professor Joyce Lishman, Head of the School of Applied Social Studies at the Robert Gordon University.

Other titles in the series

Managing Front Line Practice in Social Care
Edited by Daphne Statham
Research Highlights in Social Work 40
ISBN 1 85302 886 X

The Changing Role of Social Care
Edited by Bob Hudson
Research Highlights in Social Work 3
ISBN 1 85302 752 9

Effective Ways of Working with Children and their Families
Edited by Malcolm Hill
Research Highlights in Social Work 35
ISBN 1 85302 619 0

Women Who Offend
Edited by Gill McIvor
Research Highlights in Social Work 44
ISBN 1 84310 154 8

Reconceptualising Work with 'Carers'
New Directions for Policy and Practice
Edited by Kirsten Stalker
Research Highlights in Social Work 43
ISBN 1 84310 118 1

Risk Assessment in Social Care and Social Work
Edited by Phyllida Parsloe
Research Highlights in Social Work 36
ISBN 1 85302 689 1

Adult Day Services and Social Inclusion
Better Days
Edited by Chris Clark
Research Highlights in Social Work 39
ISBN 1 85302 887 8

Transition and Change in the Lives of People with Intellectual Disabilities
Edited by David May
Research Highlights in Social Work 38
ISBN 1 85302 863 0

RESEARCH HIGHLIGHTS IN SOCIAL WORK 45

Social Work and Evidence-Based Practice

Edited by David Smith

Jessica Kingsley Publishers
London and Philadelphia

First published in 2004 by
Jessica Kingsley Publishers
116 Pentonville Road
London N1 9JB, UK
and
400 Market Street, Suite 400
Philadelphia, PA 19106, USA
www.jkp.com

Copyright © 2004 Robert Gordon University, Research Highlights Advisory Group, School of Applied Social Studies

Library of Congress Cataloging in Publication Data
Social work and evidence-based practice / edited by David Bromfield Smith.-- 1st American pbk. ed.
p. cm. -- (Research highlights in social work ; 45)
Includes bibliographical references and index.
ISBN 1-84310-156-4 (pbk.)
1. Social service. I. Smith, David, 1947 Aug. 2- II. Series.
HV40.S6176 2004
361.3--dc22

2004009436

British Library Cataloguing in Publication Data
A CIP catalogue record for this book is available from the British Library

ISBN 1 84310 156 4

Printed and Bound in Great Britain by
Athenaeum Press, Gateshead, Tyne and Wear

Contents

List of Tables and Figures

CHAPTER 1

Introduction

Some Versions of Evidence-Based Practice

David Smith

Evidence-based practice – what it might mean, how it could be achieved, whether it ought to be aspired to – is the subject of much debate and argument in social work in Britain and in other countries where governments have committed themselves to modernising and rationalising the provision of welfare services. In Britain interest in the topic, while not itself new, has been particularly associated with the modernising agenda of the New Labour governments that came to power in 1997 and 2001. This has involved a transfer of concepts long established in medicine and allied professions to the fields of social work and social care. Among the signs of New Labour's faith in the power of evidence to improve practice in health and social care is the establishment in 1999 of the National Institute for Clinical Excellence (producing the acronym NICE, which will sound slightly sinister to readers of C.S. Lewis's *That Hideous Strength*) and, in 2001, of its more modestly funded counterpart, the Social Care Institute for Excellence (SCIE) (Fisher 2002). Social care thus followed health care in acquiring an institute for 'excellence', to be achieved by the development and dissemination of knowledge about best practice, just as the idea of evidence-based social work followed the idea of evidence-based medicine.

A commonly followed definition of the latter, from some of its best-known advocates, is as follows:

...the conscientious, explicit and judicious use of current best evidence in making decisions about the care of individual patients, based on skills which allow the doctor to evaluate both personal experience and external evidence in a systematic and objective manner. (Sackett *et al.* 1997, p.71)

Does this definition make sense for social work? It has been 'freely adapted' (see www.ex.ac.uk/cebss/) as the guiding principle of the Centre for Evidence-Based Social Services at the University of Exeter, which is partly funded by the Department of Health and partly by local authorities in the south-west of England. The director of the Centre is Brian Sheldon, probably the best-known and most consistent British advocate of the need for and feasibility of evidence-based practice in social work, and his adaptation runs: 'Evidence-based social care is the conscientious, explicit and judicious use of current best evidence in making decisions regarding the welfare of those in need' (see Sheldon and Chilvers 2002). What has disappeared from the original definition is as significant as what is retained. As Taylor and White (2002) remark, the adapted version leaves out any mention of the skills of the practitioner and the evaluation of experience; in this version of evidence-based practice, everything that counts as evidence comes from outside rather than from within the practitioner's own profes- sional experience, and there is no mention of the individual skills and qualities of the worker.

Elsewhere Sheldon has been more explicit about what might justify this exclusion; he is a long-term opponent of what he sees as fad and fashion in social work (he thinks that social work has been particularly plagued by these), and his definitions of what it means to behave in ways that are consci- entious, explicit and judicious reflect this stance (Sheldon 1998). Conscien- tious practice is practice that is not based on subjective preferences or 'favourite ideas and theories'; explicitness refers to the practitioner's ability to justify his or her decision-making procedures; and to be judicious is to choose 'helping recipes on best available evidence' and to apply them 'cautiously and within their known scope', rather than to follow trends or fashions and apply them without discrimination (Sheldon 1998, p.16).

Sheldon's metaphor of a recipe is just that, a metaphor, but it is neverthe- less revealing. Recipes come from cook-books, and can in principle be con- scientiously, explicitly and judiciously followed by anyone who can read them, with results that should be predictable and reliable. However, we know that in the practice of cookery this does not hold true, and that cooks ostensibly using the same recipe can produce very different results; the differences arise from the personal experience and skills of the cooks, and the best cooks may well deviate from the recipe in the book in order to achieve their results. To change the metaphor, a good chess-player and a poor one may have studied the same books of theory and example, but the poor player will, other things being equal, never beat the good one, because the good player not only knows the 'evidence' from books but also knows when a particular part of that evidence is relevant to the current state of play, a form of knowledge which can only be based on experience and reflection. Although medicine provides the model many advocates of evidence-based practice in social work seek to follow, the recipe approach to clinical decisions is firmly rejected by experts on the practice and teaching of evidence-based medicine: Sackett *et al.* (1997) are clear at the start of their book that they are not advocating a 'cook-book' approach. Instead they propose an integration of 'the best external evidence with individual expertise and patient choice' (p.4). It is individual expertise that enables the practitioner to decide what (if any) external evidence is relevant to the individual case and how it should be applied. The clinician who decides that some piece of evidence is not useful in this particular case will not be accused, as Sheldon accuses social workers, of irresponsibly following 'gut-feeling', whim or fashion, or of ignoring evidence in favour of theories that are irrelevant or wrong (which for Sheldon (2001) seems to include anything sociological); instead, the practitioner will be seen as acting responsibly in appropriately bringing personal experience to bear on a clinical decision. It is difficult to see what can justify the adoption in social work of exactly the kind of recipe approach to practice which is explicitly rejected by leading figures in the evidence-based movement in health care.

The point here is that in social work, as in every other practice calling for the exercise of skill and judgement, some practitioners will be better than others, and this will remain true even if all practitioners have equal access to and even equal understanding of the best external evidence. Some will still be better than others at deciding what evidence is relevant to the particular case, and what it implies for decision-making; and this superiority will be based on experience, skill and capacity for 'reflective practice' (Schön 1983). Nonetheless, this is not to suggest that practitioners should not have such access, or that they can do without such evidence and rely solely on individual judgement. Some of the earliest research on counselling and psychotherapy found that practitioners' effectiveness was related to what clients perceived as their personal qualities more than to the theories the practitioners believed themselves to be using (Truax and Carkhuff 1967). In other words, differences in these practitioners' effectiveness would need to be explained in terms of some theory of therapeutic technique, rather than by the quality of the evidence available to them, or by the truth or falsity of the theories they espoused (Keat 1981). However, this argument cuts in both directions; as Raynor (in this volume) notes, Truax and Carkhuff also found that ineffective practitioners were unconscious of their ineffectiveness; and while they tended to become even more ineffective over time, their confidence in their therapeutic prowess tended to increase. It would plainly be indefensible to leave the vulnerable and marginalised people who are the main users of social work services at the mercy of practitioners whose individual judgements are so wrong, though made with such misplaced confidence. Some external measure of effectiveness is needed, and the disquiet of Sheldon and Chilvers (2000, 2002) about social workers' apparent inability to cite any research at all that might help inform their work is well founded, even if (see below) the nature of the available evidence is more ambiguous than they would like to believe, and the question of how to use it more complex.

That it is possible to produce results that count as evidence for something, and that social workers ought to attend to such findings, are common ground among the contributors to this volume, but it is here (provided that one accepts that something worth counting as external evidence can in principle exist) that the important questions begin. For example, what is to count as evidence, and who decides this? If we can agree on what the relevant evidence is, how should we use it in practice? How can we tell, if something made a difference, what this something was (the 'black box' problem)? Should we treat apparent success in helping people change as providing evidence in support of the theory employed by the worker, or as evidence that she is a skilled, conscientious and effective worker? Is it sensible to expect something that worked well at a particular time and in a particular context to work as well at other times and in other contexts? How predictable, controlled and orderly can social work become, given that it works with problems that are often complex and capable of being rationally defined in more than one way? These are the kinds of questions addressed in the following chapters.

The poles of the argument

There are, of course, views of evidence-based practice that are not represented here. One is the position particularly associated in a British context with Brian Sheldon, whose views were quoted above. According to Sheldon and his co-believers, the only problem with evidence-based practice is that there is not enough of it about. There is no problem, in principle at least, about conducting research on effectiveness that will reveal the forms of practice that are most likely to produce desirable outcomes (and there is little or no room for argument about what counts as desirable). Where the problem arises is in the gap between 'aspiration and reality' (Sheldon and Chilvers 2002): social work practitioners are enthusiastic about the idea of evidence-based practice and think their work would be enhanced if it were guided by evidence, but, when asked, are usually unable to think of any evaluative study at all; even when the evidence is there they are unaware of it (Sheldon and Chilvers 2000). According to Sheldon and Chilvers, at least part of the blame for this should be directed at the academics with responsibility for educating students for the social work profession, because they either ignore the available evidence or, unlike prac-titioners and managers, are suspicious of the very idea of evidence-based practice.

In support of this claim about academics Sheldon and Chilvers (2002) cite Webb (2001), whose argument is close to the opposite end to Sheldon's on a continuum running from a thoroughgoing scientific empiricism to a thoroughgoing scepticism about the claims of evidence-based practice. (There may be positions beyond Webb's on this continuum; while influenced by various strands of postmodern thought, he distances himself from those postmodernists who consider that nothing is decidable and that there can be no rational grounds – merely preferences – for believing anything to be true.) Webb (2001, p.58) argues that evidence-based practice is 'deeply appealing to our contemporary technocratic culture' and presents a threat to 'traditional professional practice, whilst further legitimating a harsher managerialist ethos…in social work'. Suspicious of its ideological uses, Webb also argues that the movement for evidence-based practice rests on a misunderstanding of the nature of professional social work practice. Social workers, Webb claims, are not the rational decision-makers that the evidence-based practice movement requires them to be, and he cites evidence that in everyday life people assess probabilities and come to conclusions on the basis of heuristic rules of thumb rather than on evidence. Thus, according to Webb, the evidence-based practice movement is founded on a mistaken view of how decisions in the real world are actually – and inevitably – made.

This argument is, however, open to a serious objection. There is indeed plenty of evidence that most of the time we are not rational in the sense of using scientific evidence to inform our decisions, but, as Sheldon (2001) was quick to point out, it does not follow that social workers who have the power to make the kinds of crucial decisions that will affect the lives of service users cannot or should not approach these decisions more rationally and carefully than they do when deciding what to do in their everyday lives. Webb (p.72) himself cites the phenomenonologist Alfred Schutz: 'we do not interpret the social world…in a rational way, except under special circumstances which compel us to leave our basic attitude of just living our lives'. However, when social workers are making important decisions they are arguably in exactly such 'special circumstances', and have an obligation to think harder, more systematically, and more conscientiously about what they ought to do. Social workers, as professionals with the power to do harm as well as good, plainly ought to know if there is evidence that might help them decide in such situations; and they also ought to be able, on the basis of experience and reflection on experience, to select from the evidence what is most useful and relevant in the particular case.

Webb's root-and-branch rejection of evidence-based practice is, I am suggesting, hard to defend; but so is Sheldon's version of what evidence-based practice means, for various reasons, some of which I have already suggested. Sheldon represents what Shaw (1999, pp.15–16) calls the 'narrow-stream' version of evidence-based practice, characterised by advocacy of methodlogical rigour in evaluation (usually privileging experimental or quasi-experimental designs over other approaches) and of behavioural or cognitive-behavioural methods of intervention. Advocates of the narrow-stream version accept much of the agenda of the 'broad-stream' version, such as the need to make research findings more accessible and to promote their use in practice; but they tend to bracket off or respond impatiently to many of the questions listed above, such as who decides what evidence is to count, how it is to be used and for what purposes, and how we can assess the importance of context and process. In varying degrees narrow-stream advocates tend to regard such questions as at best distractions from the central task of establishing social work on a secure empirical (indeed scientific) basis, and at worst as disreputably motivated attempts to evade the uncomfortable duty of subjecting social work to rigorous objective assessment. They are committed to a 'scientific' paradigm for research and practice, which risks excluding all 'evidence' that has not been produced by acceptably scientific methods, and, according to some commentators, this is a paradigm that rests on a fundamental misconception of the nature of social work and indeed of the social world. Some aspects of this line of criticism are considered next.

Art and science in social work

There is no reason why critics of the evidence-based practice movement should not acknowledge that good social work practice entails the exercise of knowledge, skill and judgement in ways that are distinct from 'just living our lives'. The tradition of reflective practice, for example, represents a commitment to the rigorous use of evidence that is just as strong as that of the 'narrow-stream' of evidence-based practice, but makes room for the creativity and self-awareness of the practitioner (Schön 1983; Fook 1999). The reflective social worker uses evidence from outside her own professional and personal experience (for example, through considering what empirically grounded theories might help in understanding a pattern of family interaction), but she also treats her experience as itself a source of evidence (for example, by considering what connects the current situation with others she has encountered, how she might interpret the language being used by the family members as a way of understanding their perception of themselves and others, or how she should interpret the emotions that are aroused in her by the interaction of the family members). This process – of disciplined reflection on practice with a view to improving it – entails the exercise of faculties not easily recognised within a rigid 'scientific' approach to what counts as evidence, but to disqualify it as insufficiently scientific would be to lose an important source of social workers' capacity to develop their understanding of the complex human situations that often confront them, and hence their ability to respond to them helpfully.

Some commentators have suggested that social work has suffered not from a lack of attention to science as a model for its practice but from excessive respect for it. Writing as Latino women in the United States, Martinez-Brawley and Zorita (1998, p.197) suggest that in their professional lives the best social workers 'rely on cognitive maps that incorporate elements of art, craft and disciplined reasoning'. The argument of these authors is that, far from being a late convert to 'technical rationality' (Schön 1983), social work was inappropriately in thrall to a positivist, scientific paradigm for much of the twentieth century. Writing from a perspective that celebrates the creative and 'artistic' achievements of social work practitioners, for example in exploring ways of making psychoanalytic theory yield up social work practices that were accessible and useful to their clients, Martinez-Brawley and Zorita note that Mary Richmond, whose *Social Diagnosis* was published in 1917, was committed to establishing social work on a 'scientific' basis (and one could add that C.S. Loch, the long-serving secretary of the Charity Organisation Society in Britain, aspired to make it a 'scientific religious charity' (Woodroofe 1962)).

Not surprisingly, in trying to establish its professional credentials social work adopted the language of the sciences that had transformed social life over the course of the nineteenth century; but Martinez-Brawley (2001) argues that this was at the cost of excluding forms of understanding that could not neatly be incorporated into the discourses of science. She suggests that the dominance of the scientific paradigm until towards the end of the century marginalised those who spoke 'from the edge of the frame' – primarily, in a United States context, 'women and minorities of colour' (Martinez-Brawley 2001, p.273). Local, indigenous knowledge and ways of understanding were overlooked as social work sought to use science 'to build a framework of steel' (Martinez-Brawley and Zorita 1998, p.210) that was unsuited to the realities of social work practice, in particular to its inherently practical, concrete and contextualised character, and to its commitment to those vulnerable to economic, social and cultural exclusion. The authors cite Gergen's (1982) metaphor that contrasts the 'mighty oaks' of the natural sciences with the 'sprawling thicket' of the social and behavioural sciences, and argue that rather than trying to get the thicket under control we should accept it as a reflection of the diversity and unpredictability of social life, to which the natural science model of knowledge-building is simply not applicable. Martinez-Brawley and Zorita thus argue for a plurality of perspectives, for an acceptance of uncertainty and indeterminacy, and for respect for traditional ways of understanding the social and natural worlds. (Lest it should be thought that this represents a sentimental resistance to rationality that is unique to social work, it is worth noting that a similar recognition that there is no one right (or scientific) way of assessing 'goods' and 'bads' is gaining ground in environmental philosophy (Agrawal 1999).) Martinez-Brawley and Zorita also remind us that the scientific, rationalist approach that underpins the 'narrow-stream' understanding of evidence-based practice has the potential to exclude and ignore those whose identities come from traditions different from that of nineteenth-century positivism.

Science, order and exclusion

There seems little doubt that, in making policy, a narrowly scientific or positivist conception of evidence-based practice could be used, or at any rate that managers and bureaucrats might try to use it, in a way that privileges only one view of what counts as a good outcome and marginalises or discounts the views of 'stakeholders' whose definitions of success might be different. Science promises what managers long for: control, certainty, predictability and an end to ignorance and doubt. The idea that we actually do know what 'works' – and that this is something single, unified, measurable and visible – is therefore liable to be a highly seductive one for managers of human services, because it allows them to see the social world (and their own tasks as managers) as at least potentially orderly and predictable, and to claim a rational basis for seeking to impose a single, simple model of best practice (Smith 2002). However, there are good arguments that this dream of order and certainty can never be realised – and that attempts to realise it are, as some have argued, dangerous (Bauman 1989). The fundamental reason why the dream must remain a dream lies in the differences between the natural and social sciences. MacIntyre (1985) has argued persuasively that the social sciences cannot and should not be expected to yield the law-like generalisations that managers and policy-makers would like to draw from them. This is because the social world is inherently unpredictable and uncertain in ways that the natural world, at least in principle, is not. There is therefore no social science theory – behaviourism or anything else – from which forms of practice can be derived that will always 'work' in the same way in different contexts. While this may be bad news for bureaucrats, it need not be for social workers in search of useful theories to inform their practice, because it follows from the indeterminacy of the social sciences that theories can continue to be useful to practitioners concerned with under-standing problems and seeking solutions even if the predictions that can be derived from them sometimes or even often turn out to be incorrect when subjected to scientific analysis (Braithwaite 1993). What matters or should matter in making choices among theories is whether a given theory is helpful in a particular context (social work is always practised in a particular context) in relation to a particular problem, not whether it has consistently demonstrated its predictive power. We should, on this argument, accept that social workers, like other human service professionals, will continue to confront a sprawling thicket, rather than a tidy assemblage of well-established oaks; and this is so because of the nature of social life itself, not just because social work is an inherently messy and uncertain practice (though that is probably true too).

The thicket consists not only of social science theories that overlap and intertwine, but also of a range of ethical and political ideas whose competing claims cannot be resolved by an appeal to evidence, or to a set of values that commands universal assent, however much social workers and their managers may yearn for certainty (Hugman and Smith 1995). Perhaps the most obvious reason why this is so, is that in situations where there is some conflict of interests (which is the case in many of the situations in which social workers intervene) what is a good for one person may not be a good for another. Take the case of an older person whose behaviour has become erratic or potentially dangerous and whose relatives believe that he needs residential care, while he himself sees this as a denial of his rights and freedoms and is keen to remain in his own home. In such a situation the social worker cannot act in such a way as to promote the well-being (as they see it) of all concerned: admission to residential care will free the relatives from anxieties and responsibilities they may feel unable to sustain, but will be perceived by the older person as rejection and stigmatisation. Evidence can help the social worker decide what to do (for example, in assessing the risk of harm if the older person remains at home) but it cannot be the sole determinant of her decision about whose conception of a good outcome is to prevail. Nor can a general ethical commitment to empowerment or maximisation of choice tell her who in this situation should be empowered and given choices, and who should be disempowered and denied the opportunity to choose. The virtues of the good social worker (MacIntyre 1985; Hugman and Smith 1995; McBeath and Webb 2002) certainly include a conscientious commitment to making helpful use of evidence, but they also include (for example) fairness in judging between competing goods, honesty towards service users and to oneself, and care and compassion for the suffering and vulnerable.

Who decides what is evidence, and what evidence matters?

Questions about what is to count as evidence, and what it is evidence of, are inherently disputable, and this is recognised by, among others, researchers who have themselves made important contributions to evidence-based practice. For example, Drakeford (2000, p.524) cites a seminar paper by Gill McIvor in which she noted the tension between evidence-based practice and a commitment to attending seriously to service users' views, and argued that the emphasis on evidence-based practice risked devaluing these views, encouraging an over-restrictive view of what evidence is, and giving priority to the outcomes and definitions of effectiveness that are of most interest to policy-makers. Similarly, Phillips and Blyth (2000) cite a paper by David Gibbs (from the same series of seminars on 'Theorising Social Work Research', which was funded by the Economic and Social Research Council in 1999–2000) in which he questioned whether the evidence-based practice movement was compatible with authentic engagement in the research process of service users. There is a case for saying that social work as a research discipline has been in the forefront of attempts to involve service users in setting the research agenda and to use research to promote the social inclusion of disadvantaged groups and 'in listening to children, researching sensitive topics and theorizing diversity' (Mullender 2000, pp.426–7; for examples of this and related perspectives on research see Dullea and Mullender 1999; Evans and Fisher 1999; Humphries 1999). If the evidence-based practice movement were to sweep all before it, arguably much that has been distinctive about social work research – its interest in developing understandings of research that are in line with the practical and ethical commitments of social work practice – would be lost.

The disabled people's movement has been especially active and successful in efforts to ensure that the perspectives of service users are incorporated into the research process (Beresford 2000), and in this volume Bob Sapey's contribution probably provides the clearest example of how in the real world evidence of good practice can mean very different things to different people – in this case, to the managers of community care resources and to the disabled people for whose benefit the resources supposedly exist. What managers see as a satisfactory outcome may be far from satisfactory from the viewpoint of the users – or would-be users – of the service. Claire Taylor's chapter, too, stresses the importance, in defining what are to count as good outcomes, of attending to those whose voices have often gone unheard in the places where policy is made and resources allocated – in this case, to looked-after children. The contributors to this volume deal with a variety of topics and present a range of perspectives on what the relevant evidence is, how it is or might be used to inform practice, and how it relates to the political and professional contexts in which practitioners work; but all, I think, would accept that the arguments outlined above mean that claims made on behalf of evidence-based practice should be modest and provisional rather than triumphalist, that uncertainty will remain ineradicably present in any social work intervention, and that positivist rationality should not be allowed to silence other forms of understanding and interpreting the world.

Why getting good evidence is difficult

Even if one adopts the 'narrow-stream' position on what counts as valid evidence, the process of acquiring evidence that is good enough to deserve to be used is more difficult than the advocates of a positivist, scientific approach make it sound. There is also a sense in several of the contributions here of the sheer difficulty and complexity of the task of producing helpful evidence and determining how to use it. Peter Raynor cites the finding that in the probation service in England and Wales, several years after a commitment to 'what works' had become well established, it was very rare for programmes to be subjected to any kind of evaluation at all. Raynor treats this as an indication that the virtues of local autonomy have been exaggerated, and that practitioners, left to their own devices, will not bother with evaluating their work. One reason why they apparently fail to do so is that evaluation (at least evaluation with enough rigour to be useful) is inherently difficult (that it is so, any honest evaluator will testify).

Part of the difficulty arises from the 'black box' problem – if something made a difference, can we tell what it was? – that has been the focus of attention by 'realist' evaluators (Pawson and Tilley 1997). Knowing what it was that made a difference, if something did, requires close attention to the processes – or 'mechanisms', in Pawson and Tilley's terms – that may have produced the observable outcomes. The study of processes is necessarily time-consuming, labour-intensive and intellectually demanding, since it requires close and repeated observation, followed by the development of hypotheses about which elements of the practice being observed are crucial for success. Since it would be unethical to test these hypotheses experimentally – by changing or removing some hypothetically helpful aspect of practice to see if doing so makes things worse – they can only be tested by exploring how well they fit with the theories about the intervention held by practitioners and service users. Conclusions about the truth of the hypotheses – for example, that in working with offenders or people suffering from depression what is important is to use cognitive–behavioural methods – will necessarily be tentative and provisional, until they are supported by studies of a range of interventions using these methods. The process of acquiring evidence good enough to justify a claim that we have identified the most effective forms of practice is necessarily a slow and incremental one.

The difficulty of determining what made the difference, if something did, is increased because social work interventions cannot sensibly be abstracted from the specific environment in which they are undertaken. The environment in this sense includes, at a minimum, the available resources, the degree of management support for the intervention, the quality of the staff involved, and the support or lack of it that the intervention receives from other agencies (for the importance of inter-agency co-operation see Colin Pritchard's second chapter in this volume, and the contribution of Julie Taylor-Browne). It will always be difficult, and sometimes impossible, to be certain (as opposed to cautiously optimistic) that it was specifically the social work intervention that made the difference, rather than some other change in the life of service users (in employment, education, health, relations with family and friends, drug use, and so on). The importance of the environment of interventions also means that, strictly speaking, replication of a successful intervention in another place and at another time is impossible (Pawson and Tilley 1997): there will always be enough difference in the context of the intervention to allow for the possibility that some crucial environmental element will be absent, or so changed as to have lost its capacity to make the difference (obvious candidates are the quality and commitment of the staff, and the degree of effective support from other agencies).

Finally, it is worth remarking that even apparently 'hard' outcome data are often more problematic to interpret than 'narrow stream' enthusiasts tend to allow. Cheetham *et al.* (1992), fully aware of the difficulties of getting satisfactory measures of change in the desired direction in many fields of social work, treat reconvictions for criminal offences following some social work intervention as harder data than most; but, as Mair *et al.* (1997) have argued, and as anyone who has used reconvictions as an outcome measure can confirm, this superficially 'hard' measure tends to soften under close scrutiny. Even if the sources of reconviction statistics were completely reliable (which they are not), there would still be problems in using and interpreting them, most obviously because reconviction is not the same as reoffending. Other problems include: when one should start counting (from the start or the end of the intervention?); how long one should keep counting (what should the follow-up period be?); and what counts as success (is any reconviction an indicator of failure, or should fewer or less serious convictions than before the intervention count as success?). If there are such problems with an ostensibly clear either/or measure such as reconviction, the difficulties are likely to be greater when the measures of success are less clear-cut. For example, what outcomes would count as evidence of good practice in work with looked-after children? And how long-term would these outcomes need to be? Ideally, one might want to follow up these children well into their adult lives, but the resources required for such a study mean that long-term follow-ups are rare; there have, for example, only ever been two studies (both American) that have tracked children subject to early intervention even up to the age of 15 (Karoly *et al.* 1998). Readers are invited to think for themselves of the range of possible measures of success that would provide evidence for good practice in other fields of social work, and to consider which measures might be favoured by which interested parties (for example, service users, their families and friends, social work practitioners, social work managers, financial controllers or policy-makers). Even if some yardstick can be agreed on, for instance indicators of social coping and well-being among mental health service users, there will still be questions that admit of no straightforward answers, such as how much improvement counts as success, how long (once again) the measure should continue, and (increasingly important) whether the intervention whose impact is being assessed represents value for money.

The contents of this book

The authors of the following chapters might disagree about much, but they share a sense of the difficulties of getting and using evidence that can helpfully inform practice. The chapters are roughly divided into two groups – those that present evidence, from the authors' own work and elsewhere, from which inferences about good practice might be drawn, and those that explore contextual and definitional issues about the nature or use of the evidence in different areas of social work practice. Chapter 2, by Jan Fook, explores what professionals need from research in a context in which the movement for evidence-based practice is only one of the global influences currently reshaping the social work profession. Fook argues that, in the face of challenges to social work's knowledge base, its legitimacy as a profession, and the values that have informed its practice, the kind of research which will be most useful will allow for the development of transferable knowledge, enhance the social contribution of the profession, and attend to the need for accountability. With these aims in view, Fook introduces the idea of research as a translation exercise, in which not only the content of the research but also the language and style in which its findings are communi- cated become important – a salutary message both for researchers prone to complain, as they are, that their work is not received with the respectful attention it deserves, and for practitioners prone to complain that social work is undervalued and misunderstood.

Chapters 3 and 4 are both by Colin Pritchard, but present very different kinds of evidence of successful social work practice. The first takes high-level data on homicides of children and draws comparisons over both time and space. Pritchard charts changes over time for each of the countries selected for analysis and compares the rates across countries. From these comparisons he concludes that the child protection services in England and Wales are among the most effective (and the most improved) in the world, but that they could be more effective still with better inter-professional com- munication – one of Jan Fook's themes, and a recurrent one in the next three chapters. The first of these is Chapter 4, Colin Pritchard's account of his research on a collaborative project between social work and education services which aimed to reduce truancy, delinquency and school exclusions in a socially deprived area. Again, using an approach that allows for comparisons over time and place, Pritchard concludes that the project was successful in increasing attachment to school, reducing delinquency, and supporting parents. He stresses the importance of the support the project received from its immediate environment and of the accessibility of the project team to both children and parents. As well as providing a detailed account of the research process, the chapter ought to be a reminder of the value of school-based social work, an underdeveloped area of practice in Britain, despite evidence (neglected during the period when the received wisdom was that 'nothing works') of its success in reducing delinquency and related problems (Rose and Marshall 1974).

Chapter 5, by Julie Taylor-Browne, also stresses the importance of inter-agency working, in this case in responding effectively to violence against women in the home, but its central message is perhaps that, while research has produced evidence which could be used to develop more effective work, this has not had the impact on practice that it should have had. The evidence is there, but not acted upon. Among the reasons Taylor-Browne suggests for this failure to pursue the implications of the evidence are that multi-agency working is perceived as so difficult that it is never properly attempted, that initiatives that are undertaken are not evaluated, and that the wishes of survivors of domestic violence, and their experiences of services, are not adequately attended to, with the result that appropriate services are not developed, and existing, sometimes inappropriate services, are under-used. Thus, a failure to attend to an important source of evidence contributes to a continued failure to translate the available evidence into improvements in practice.

Chapter 6, by authors working in the research department of the drugs charity Lifeline, also stresses the importance of 'joined-up' approaches to complex problems. It shows that, despite the salience of drug use among young people as a social problem, and the attention and resources given to the issue by successive governments, relatively little is known about what interventions are likely to be most effective with which groups. Epidemiological evidence strongly suggests that drug use among young people has continued to spread, though the authors note the limitations of the self-report studies which are the source of much of this evidence. Risk factors for problem drug use are better understood than protective factors, and evidence on effective interventions comes mainly from the United States. Nevertheless, young people's drug use has become better understood, and interventions need no longer be based on the naïve assumptions that most young people would rather not take drugs (including alcohol), and that those already taking them would like to stop; and since drug use is bound up with other aspects of young people's leisure pursuits, services should not focus on the substance being used, but on the young people using it. The growth of understanding on the part of practitioners is a good example of the use of evidence gradually and incrementally acquired, much of it, in this case, from actual and potential users of services.

Claire Taylor's chapter (7) draws on her own qualitative research on formerly looked-after children and the relationship between care experiences and criminal careers. Taylor is critical of the taken-for-granted view found in much of the relevant literature that care experiences are inherently and inevitably going to produce negative outcomes in later life. Her work is an example of how careful and respectful listening to young people can overturn widespread assumptions and lead to proposals for changes in practice. She does indeed report findings that support the view that being looked after can, in some circumstances, increase the likelihood of a prolonged delinquent career, but she also stresses that 'care' can mean very different things, and that for some young people the experience was positive and helpful. This was so when policy and practice allowed for long-term relationships and consistent attachments to be formed. The setting in which this is most likely to happen is long-term foster care, but Taylor is also critical of the view of residential care as a last, desperate resort from which no positive outcomes can be expected. She presents a persuasive argument for a more optimistic, ambitious perspective on what care can offer looked-after children, and highlights the potentially crucial role of the social worker in providing a long-term relationship of support and encouragement when there are few if any other possibilities of long-term attachments in children's lives.

Bob Sapey's chapter (8) begins by asking two questions: whether it is meaningful to define effective practice in work with disabled people without first agreeing on what the aims of intervention are; and who can and should produce the evidence that would allow effective practice to be identified. Sapey suggests that, to be useful to practitioners, research must be informed by a social (rather than a medical or individual) model of disability, attend to the ways in which social institutions have disabling effects, and help social workers overcome negative perceptions of disability. These are the characteristics of emancipatory research, much of it produced by disabled people, and conducted in the field of disability studies rather than of social work specifically. Sapey argues that the aims of policy towards disabled people tend to focus on the retention of control over resources rather than on the promotion of independent living; bureaucratic definitions of 'success' are therefore likely to differ drastically from the definitions of disabled people themselves, and practitioners become implicated in this further process of disablement. This chapter raises the question of whether social work is an appropriate form of intervention in disabled people's lives, and suggests that a positive answer is possible only if social workers can change their attitudes in such a way that they define success in terms of the outcomes of intervention for disabled people, rather than for social services departments' resources.

Peter Raynor's chapter (9) discusses the development of the movement for evidence-based practice in the probation service in England and Wales, and various ways in which the implications of the relevant evidence have been misunderstood. Raynor insists that on both ethical and practical grounds probation work needs to be informed by evidence of 'what works', and that this does not entail an uncritical abandonment of concern for the personal and social disadvantages many offenders experience, or an unwarranted optimism that a single right answer has been found for all offenders and their problems. Raynor argues that much criticism of the evidence-based practice movement in probation rests on mistaken beliefs about what the evidence actually implies, and in particular on an empirically hard-to-defend nostalgia for a supposedly better era, in which probation officers' practice was not encumbered by expectations that it be demonstrably effective. While recognising that exaggerated claims can be and have been made for what the evidence from research implies for practice, and that managerial enthusiasm can overstep the bounds of rationality, Raynor shows that even evidence that carries an ostensibly positive message – that some things work, rather than that nothing does – can produce suspicion and resistance to change. The evidence that is increasingly informing probation practice has, once again, been accumulated over years and from a variety of settings, and Raynor makes a strong case that its implications for practice are being carefully and responsibly explored.

The following chapters, then, cover both areas of social work practice in which the principles of evidence-based practice are well established and areas in which evidence is just beginning to become available. They explore different sources of evidence, obtained by different methods, and the varying relationships between evidence, policy and practice. They discuss how evidence can be used and misused, how it can be helpfully or unhelpfully disseminated, and how it can strengthen or undermine social work's moral and political commitments. They demonstrate why evidence-based practice is important, and why it is also important to think clearly and carefully about its implications for the social work profession, and for the users of social work services. I would like to thank all the contributors for their work, and believe that they have produced a rich resource for practitioners, policy-makers, researchers and users of research in social work.

References

Agrawal, A. (1999) 'On power and indigenous knowledge.' In D.A. Posey (ed.) *Cultural and Spiritual Values of Biodiversity.* London: Intermediate Technology Publications.

Bauman, Z. (1989) *Modernity and the Holocaust.* Cambridge: Polity Press.

Beresford, P. (2000) 'Service users' knowledges and social work theory: Conflict or collaboration?' *British Journal of Social Work 30,* 4, 489–503.

Braithwaite, J. (1993) 'Beyond positivism: Learning from contextual integrated strategies.' *Journal of Research in Crime and Delinquency 30,* 4, 383–399.

Cheetham, J., Fuller, R., McIvor, G. and Petch, A. (1992) *Evaluating Social Work Effectiveness.* Buckingham: Open University Press.

Drakeford, M. (2000) 'Researching social work as a means of social inclusion – notes on the Edinburgh seminar.' *British Journal of Social Work 30,* 4, 523–526.

Dullea, K. and Mullender, A. (1999) 'Evaluation and empowerment.' In I. Shaw and J. Lishman (eds) *Evaluation and Social Work Practice.* London: Sage.

Evans, C. and Fisher, M. (1999) 'Collaborative evaluation with service users.' In I. Shaw and J. Lishman (eds) *Evaluation and Social Work Practice.* London: Sage.

Fisher, M. (2002) 'The Social Care Institute for Excellence: The role of a national institute in developing knowledge and practice in social care.' *Social Work and Social Sciences Review 10,* 2, 6–34.

Gergen, K.J. (1982) *Towards Transformation in Social Knowledge.* New York: Springer-Verlag.

Fook, J. (1999) 'Critical reflectivity in education and practice.' In B. Pease and J. Fook (eds) *Transforming Social Work Practice.* London: Routledge.

Hugman, R. and Smith, D. (1995) 'Ethical issues in social work: An overview.' In R. Hugman and D. Smith (eds) *Ethical Issues in Social Work.* London: Routledge.

Humphries, B. (1999) 'Feminist evaluation.' In I. Shaw and J. Lishman (eds) *Evaluation and Social Work Practice*. London: Sage.

Karoly, L.A., Greenwood, P.W., Everingham, S.S., Houbé, J., Kilburn, M.R., Rydell, C.P., Sanders, M. and Chiesa, J. (1998) *Investing in our Children: What We Know and Don't Know about the Costs and Benefits of Early Childhood Interventions*. Santa Monica, CA: RAND Corporation.

Keat, R. (1981) *The Politics of Social Theory: Habermas, Freud and the Critique of Positivism*. Oxford: Basil Blackwell.

McBeath, G. and Webb, S. (2002) 'Virtue ethics and social work: Being lucky, realistic, and not doing one's duty.' *British Journal of Social Work 32*, 8, 1015–1036.

MacIntyre, A. (1985) *After Virtue: A Study in Moral Theory* (2nd edn). London: Duckworth.

Mair, G., Lloyd, C. and Hough, M. (1997) 'The limitations of reconviction rates.' In G. Mair (ed.) *Evaluating the Effectiveness of Community Penalties*. Aldershot: Avebury.

Martinez-Brawley, E.E. (2001) 'Searching again and again. Inclusion, heterogeneity and social work research.' *British Journal of Social Work 31*, 2, 271–285.

Martinez-Brawley, E.E. and Zorita, P.M-B. (1998) 'At the edge of the frame: Beyond science and art in social work.' *British Journal of Social Work 28*, 2, 197–212.

Mullender, A. (2000) 'Editorial.' *British Journal of Social Work 30*, 4, 425–427.

Pawson, R. and Tilley, N. (1997) *Realistic Evaluation*. London: Sage.

Phillips, J. and Blyth, E. (2000) 'Who owns the research process? Notes on the Belfast Seminar.' *British Journal of Social Work 30*, 4, 519–522.

Rose, G. and Marshall, T.F. (1974) *Counselling and School Social Work*. London: Wiley.

Sackett, D.L., Richardson, S., Rosenberg, W. and Haynes, R.B. (1997) *Evidence-based Medicine: How to Practise and Teach EBM*. Edinburgh: Churchill Livingstone.

Schön, D.A. (1983) *The Reflective Practitioner*. New York: Basic Books.

Shaw, I. (1999) 'Evidence for Practice.' In I. Shaw and J. Lishman (eds) *Evaluation and Social Work Practice*. London: Sage.

Sheldon, B. (1998) 'Evidence-based social services: Prospects and problems.' *Research Policy and Planning 16*, 2, 16–18.

Sheldon, B. (2001) 'The validity of evidence-based practice: A reply to Stephen Webb.' *British Journal of Social Work 31*, 6, 801–809.

Sheldon, B. and Chilvers, R. (2000) *Evidence-based Social Care: A Study of Prospects and Problems*. Lyme Regis: Russell House.

Sheldon, B. and Chilvers, R. (2002) 'An empirical study of the obstacles to evidence-based practice.' *Social Work and Social Sciences Review 10*, 1, 6–26.

Smith, D. (2002) 'The limits of positivism revisited.' *Social Work and Social Sciences Review 10*, 1, 27–37.

Taylor, C. and White, S. (2002) 'What works about what works? Fashion, fad and EBP.' *Social Work and Social Sciences Review 10*, 2, 63–81.

Truax, C. and Carkhuff, R. (1967) *Towards Effective Counseling and Psychotherapy*. New York: Aldine.

Webb, S. (2001) 'Some considerations on the validity of evidence-based practice in social work.' *British Journal of Social Work 31*, 1, 57–79.

Woodroofe, K. (1962) *From Charity to Social Work in England and the United States*. London: Routledge and Kegan Paul.

CHAPTER 2

What Professionals Need from Research

Beyond Evidence-Based Practice

Jan Fook

What do professionals need from research? A few decades ago this might have been a relatively simple question to answer, but in more recent times the idea of professionalism is undergoing renewed debate in response to social and economic changes (Rossiter 1996; Shapiro 2000). In addition, the idea of research is expanding and becoming more complex as ideas about the nature of knowledge and knowledge-generation develop. To examine in detail what professionals need from research, we need to some extent to review the meaning of professionalism, and the sorts of contributions research can make in developing notions of effective professionalism and professional practice in relation to the current climate.

In this chapter my main aim is to draw up a research agenda for professionals in the light of changes in the current context. I start from the premise that the evidence-based practice movement, although representing a major recent change, is nevertheless only one particular manifestation of changes which affect current professional practice. To gain a comprehensive picture of research directions which are needed we need to understand this movement in the context of other and broader changes. In this chapter I try to link some directions for professional research with this broad context of changes, which will help us map future pathways for professionalism.

I begin by outlining how current economic, workplace and social changes influence expectations of professional practice, and how expectations of professional knowledge and accountability must change accordingly. I then use this discussion to draw up a framework for guiding the contribution of research for professionals. Where appropriate I include examples of types of research approaches, studies, designs, and methods which might meet these needs.

What does it mean to be a professional?

The idea of professions

Traditional 'trait' approaches to defining the professions characterise them as including a series of indispensable features: being founded on a mission of service; the use of a specialist and definable body of knowledge and set of skills; and the regulation of entry to the professional group by a professional body (Greenwood 1957). Using this functionalist set of criteria (Shapiro 2000), it seems a relatively simple task to distinguish between, and accord differing status to, different occupational groupings depending on the number of such features they exhibit.

However, this highlights the idea of another perspective on the professions, which recognises that professions are also defined in status terms (Johnson 1970; Parry and Parry 1976; Hugman 1991): an important part of their definition lies in their ability to lay claim to and control a body of specialist knowledge, which in turn legitimates their social position. How professions produce and use this knowledge to maintain their status within changing social and economic contexts becomes a major issue. The process of professionalisation can therefore be seen as a process of defining, laying claim to, and controlling a distinct body of knowledge and skills, or expertise.

What is common to both these perspectives is that professionalism does involve a number of key elements – a knowledge dimension, a value dimension, and a control dimension – although the discourse about them may vary. Because of the service dimension, professions embody an imperative to apply or practise their knowledge in a way which benefits the societies or communities which provide their mandate. Neither of these perspectives in fact excludes the other: the particular features of professions might perform many different functions, legitimating the status of the professional at the same time as serving a community group. In some cases one might depend upon the other.

In this chapter I take what might be termed a type of postmodern view of professions – that professionalism *per se* is not necessarily about either the pursuit of status or the 'innocent' provision of service. There might in fact be many instances in which the same activity can function in contradictory ways, or in complementary ways for different groups: it is difficult to control or even predict the many differing effects of one piece of action. In this context, then, what is important is that processes of professionalisation, and professional activities generally, attempt to contribute to building up relevant knowledge, and bettering both professional and service user positions in collaborative rather than competitive ways. In my view professional legitimation and the provision of better services are not necessarily mutually exclusive endeavours.

In this type of view, what become the more important questions for professionals are not whether they are in general terms preserving their own status or serving the interests of service users, but how and whether specific knowledges and practices can function to serve the interests of specific service users at any one time. These types of questions are becoming much more difficult to answer in the current context of changes.

Current challenges

What characterises the current contexts in which professionals work? It is commonly recognised that, with processes of globalisation, practice takes place in more complex, uncertain and changing environments. Ironically, with the increased economic and technological 'compressing' (Robertson 1992) of the world through globalisation, there is a related 'fragmentation' of old cultural, political and geographic structures, and in this climate of change the uncertainty of our social world and its interactions is increasingly acknowledged. This uncertainty means that the ability of professionals to practise effectively on the basis of tried and tested knowledge is undermined considerably.

Some of the economic changes associated with globalisation produce increased competition (Dominelli 1996). This increased competition leads to a more managerialised and technocratised workplace, both adding up to an increasing deprofessionalisation. In order for services to remain competitive they must be measurable and marketable. This means that professional specialist ownership of bodies of knowledge and skills which are value-based are seen as non-competitive in a global market. In order to develop competitive services, managers seek to break down and challenge professional ownership of knowledge and skill domains. If such expertise can be delivered in smaller discrete packages by less qualified people, or by machines, it can be marketed more cheaply and in greater economies of scale.

By the same token, jobs are framed in more fragmented and programme-defined ways. For example, Parton (1998) talks about how social *workers* are now seen as case *managers*, involved in tasks such as assessing need and risk and delivering packages of care, rather than as case *workers* using therapeutic skills in human relationships. In Australia, deprofessionalisation is manifesting itself in more short-term, contract and low-wage employment (MacDonald 2000), and in the employment of professionals such as social workers in jobs which are either not defined as social work positions, or which only require a lower level of qualification (Hawkins *et al.* 2000).

This increasing deprofessionalisation and technocratisation of skills has led to 'border skirmishes' and competition between professions and disciplines, many wanting to claim exclusive or dominant expertise in newly defined skill areas such as case management (Fook 2002, pp.149–150). The ability to practise in interdisciplinary or multidisciplinary ways has therefore become important in capturing new skill areas.

There are related social and cultural changes as well. It is widely acknowledged that the changes of globalisation are associated with postmodern thinking (Parton 1994). These changes have called into question the nature of knowledge and the legitimate forms of its generation, up-ending the traditional hierarchical divisions between, on the one hand, generalisable and tested theory developed through 'scientific research' produced by elite researchers and, on the other, everyday practice knowledge generated and changed through concrete interactions and experiences of 'ordinary' people. This thinking clearly challenges the position of the professional as the privileged keeper of specialist knowledge, and the right of the professional to develop and define what is to count as valid knowledge. Moreover, postmodernism recognises the *interpretive* (Ife 1995, p.131) and *reflective* (Fook 1996) nature of knowledge, both perspectives challenging the idea that professional knowledge is necessarily 'objective' and unchangeable.

A related pressure is a disaffection with 'professional dominance' (Friedson 1970) and the call for professions to be more accountable and transparent in their dealings. The move towards evidence-based practice (EBP) can be seen as part of this trend. Although perspectives on what evidence-based practice actually entails may vary (Trinder 2000), it is safe to say that there is broad agreement that the movement hopes to ensure that professional practice is based on the best available knowledge of what constitutes effective methods. Whether or not enough or appropriate knowledge exists to constitute 'evidence' is another question. Because the EBP movement partly originated in a concern with the gap between clinical practice and research in medicine (Reynolds 2000), the discourse about EBP often assumes the rhetoric about research in this discipline. Hence some people may interpret the EBP push as associated with the pressure for professional practice to become more technologised (Rolfe 2000, p.196), and for professional practice research to be more positivistic and measurement-based. The debates about EBP in this sense may be caught up with the debates about different research paradigms and their appropriateness for professional practice research.

The concern with EBP is part of a much bigger debate about the types of thinking and approaches to research which are most relevant for professional practice. As I have argued earlier, these debates are tied to our understanding of current social, cultural and economic changes on a global scale. In order for us as professionals to be more effective and responsive in our broader context, it is important that we also engage with these larger-scale debates, and not be restricted to the framework of the evidence-based practice movement. This is particularly important for professions outside medicine, because of the need to frame the debate in terms which are relevant to their own professions.

Let us summarise the broad dilemmas which arise for professionals in the current context. They involve three main themes:

1. The need to practise effectively in uncertain and complex contexts when the possibility and desirability of certain and unchangeable knowledge are also called into question.

2. The concern to provide value-based service in an increasingly technocratised environment.

3. The need to maintain position and credibility in an environment calling for increased accountability and transparency.

What professionals need therefore in the current environment is a legitimate form of knowledge, and legitimate forms of generating knowledge, which allow for effective and responsive practice in changing, complex and uncertain environments. In addition, they need to be able to provide service in technocratised terms, but also to relate these technologies to service values and ideals. Third, they need to be able to establish and maintain their legitimacy in order to retain some influence on the way services are delivered – which should not be at the expense of service users or the community or even other professional groups.

With these themes in mind, the concern for evidence-based practice can be framed as part of a broader need; professionals need to find ways of researching and understanding their practice knowledge in both *responsive* and *responsible* ways. The need in this sense is for responsive and *responsible* practice – this includes the use of evidence, but it also includes the imperative to match professional practice and knowledge with the situation at hand. This is both a more extensive and a much more complex idea than the use of evidence in practice.

A concept of professional expertise

It is difficult to imagine what specific forms such responsive and responsible professional practice might take. Is it possible to frame an understanding of our expertise in ways that take account of complexities, situational changes, and precarious political tensions and interests? In this section I digress slightly to look in more detail at how these sorts of challenges might affect our notions of what is involved in professional practice and expertise. I include this section because I believe it will assist in developing a more detailed understanding of the directions our research should take. I draw this material from an extensive recent study I undertook with some colleagues (Fook, Ryan and Hawkins 2000) on the actual practice of social and community development workers. The research attempted both to identify some characteristics of professional expertise based on specific accounts of practice, and to frame these characteristics in ways which addressed these challenges (Fook 2000). The main features which emerged are examined below.

Contextuality is a major feature of professional expertise. This refers to the ability to work in and with the whole context or situation. This ability requires a knowledge of how differing and competing factors influence a situation. In this sense the main focus of the professional's attention is the whole context, rather than specific aspects or players within it. The expert professional simply assumes that the pathway to understanding is to understand the whole context, and the different perspectives which are part and parcel of this. Similarly, the pathway to relevant practice is through working with the whole context. This orientation of contextuality involves a type of *connectedness*, as discussed by Belenky *et al.* (1986, p.113), in which the knower recognises the need to connect with the viewpoints and experiences of others on the road to self-knowledge and learning.

Knowledge and theory creation are related to contextuality in that they involve the ability to generate knowledge and theory which is relevant to changing contexts. This means that professionals are constantly engaged with situations in such a way that they are not just modifying existing knowledge, but are in fact creating new knowledge which is relevant to newly experienced and often changing situations. As Eraut (1994, p.54) points out, the skill of using knowledge relevantly in a particular situation involves the skill of creating new knowledge about how to do this. The ability to create new knowledge relevant to context is a skill which can therefore readily be transferred across contexts. The feature of *transferability* is therefore *a major alternative to that of generalisability.* What becomes important to the practitioner is the extent to which knowledge can be transferred, and made contextually *relevant rather than generalisable*. In more modernist conceptions, abstract generalised theories are deductively applied to make sense of newly encountered situations. Existing meanings are imposed. In a more postmodern conception, meaning is created inductively from the experience at hand. There is a sense of uncertainty about this:

> …there is certainty yet I am comfortable with uncertainty…I have gone from uncertainty and hesitation about my role to developing confidence in that role…but also at the same time, to live with uncertainty, which is OK and good; if you stay uncertain, you'll stay striving towards… (Fook *et al.* 2000, Chapter 9)

Since the creation of meaning becomes an important skill, this places emphasis on the *processual* nature of professional expertise. Practitioners generally do not foreclose on interpretations or outcomes. Instead, practice and theory are often mutually negotiated with the players in the situation. This openness to the service user's experience, and the engaging in a process which enables them to communicate it, is related to the decision of some experienced workers not to use preconceived theory, but rather to try to remain as open to the situation as possible and to 'play it by ear'. It was as if they were willing to risk uncertainty, for the sake of constructing the most relevant process and outcome for service users. One worker states, in relation to her sense of social work theory: 'each person is creating their own…useful practice is allowing clients to experience their own paradoxes and contradictions' (Fook *et al.* 2000, Chapter 7).

If knowledge and theory creation are integral features of professional expertise then skills of *reflexivity and critical reflexivity* are also involved. Reflexivity, in one sense, is related to the skill of theory creation as embodied in the *reflective process* first discussed by Argyris and Schön (1974). They argued that theory is embedded in practice, and that practitioners therefore develop theory inductively out of ongoing experience. It is this theory which can be articulated and better developed through a reflective process. Professional expertise therefore involves the ability to reflect upon, and develop theory from, practice. However, reflexivity refers also to the ability to locate oneself squarely within a situation, and to know and take into account the influence of personal interpretation, position and action within a specific context. Expert practitioners are reflexive in that they are self-knowing and responsible actors, rather than detached observers. They are *critically reflexive* if they also hold a commitment to challenging power relations and arrangements (Fook 1999).

A tension that practitioners grapple with is how to retain meaning and a broader sense of purpose when contexts change, and are often contradictory. How do expert practitioners maintain the will to constantly recreate theory, and keep themselves open to new situations, all the while juggling conflicts? How do we keep the faith to attain a collective 'good', at the same time not foreclosing on what that good might be by incorporating diverse and conflicting perspectives?

An answer perhaps lies in a pathway that many of our experienced practitioners had forged. Experts appear to subscribe to a broader level of values which transcends the immediate workplace. It may take the form of a commitment to the profession, to social justice ideals, or to a system of humanitarian and social values. Elsewhere this has been termed a 'calling' (Gustafson 1982), which encapsulates the moral vision of professions like social work. This commitment to a higher order of values allows workers to maintain a *grounded yet transcendent* vision. It allows them to be fully aware of, and responsive to, the daily conflicts of practice situations, yet also allows them to pursue broader goals which make the daily dilemmas meaningful. It might be said that they have developed a construct of professional social work expertise which allows for uncertainty and conflict, and also for a sense of ultimate direction. They are aware of constraints, but, like some of the students in Hindmarsh's study (1992, p.232), are not disempowered by this awareness. They can act as involved and participating players because they have a meaning system which makes it worthwhile.

In summary,

> …expert professionals are grounded in specific contexts [and] relate to the
> whole context… They interact, reflexively and responsively in these contexts,
> recognising multiple viewpoints, conflicts and complexities. As flexible prac
> titioners…they engage in a process…using a range of skills… They use this
> knowledge creatively, from diverse sources, and are able to relate and create
> this knowledge in the specific context, and thus transfer it relevantly to other
> contexts. Although grounded in specific contexts, they are able to transcend
> the constraints of these because…their broader vision gives them meaning

and a sense of continuity…they are therefore able to deal with uncertainty by maintaining a higher order of meaning which is flexible enough to adapt and respond to continual change. (Fook *et al.*. 2000, p.97)

What professionals need

How do these ideas of professional expertise square up against the current dilemmas which professionals face? From our earlier section it is possible to summarise the current situation as involving a crisis on three counts: knowledge, values and legitimacy.

It appears that professional expertise, as practised by current professionals, already involves the ability to use and develop knowledge in a flexible way in order to practise effectively in changing and uncertain situations. They can also learn to transfer relevant knowledge between contexts. Expert professionals are also able to maintain a sense of values, of ongoing mission and service, despite the particular challenges to this in the specific job. What is less developed from the above material are the ways in which professional expertise can be both legitimated and remain accountable in a changing economic and community context.

We need a research agenda, therefore, which recognises and continues to identify the ways in which professionals create and develop relevant and flexible knowledge through their own practice. We also need research which showcases the ways in which professionals maintain their value base and sense of mission, and which indeed contributes to this mission. Last, we need research which can legitimate our work in a number of new and different ways.

A research agenda for professionals

The above discussion indicates a number of major ways in which research can contribute to the developing position of professionals in the current climate. I have grouped the research directions into five main types, picking up the themes discussed above. I discuss the research directions needed around knowledge development and transferability of knowledge. With regard to the issue of maintaining a mission of service, I discuss the need for professional research to make a social contribution. In relation to the need for legitimation, I discuss both legitimation and accountability, as I believe the issues go hand in hand. Last, I outline research directions related to workplace development, as they involve changing notions of professional practice as defined by labour market changes.

Knowledge development

To respond to the current demands for accountability in a changing environment, the development of professional knowledge involves two major needs: to ensure that standards are maintained and that practice is improved. As noted earlier, these are the concerns of the EBP movement, yet there are more complex issues at stake as well as the need to ground practice in proven methods. It is one thing to provide clear data or 'evidence' in situations which are known and testable. It is a far more complex task to ensure standards and improvement in situations which are new and relatively unresearched or 'unresearchable'.

Therefore one of the directions research in the area of professional knowledge development needs to take is to focus on areas which are relatively under-researched and which might traditionally have been regarded as unresearchable, or difficult to measure or identify. These might include practice with complexities (Gibbs 2001), value-based practice, or holistic practice. Research on the tacit aspects of 'practice wisdom' is both particularly difficult and particularly important (Scott 1990; Fook 2001). Some examples of such research might include evaluations which include a range of methods (ranging from 'subjective' to 'objective'); studies which focus on the types of knowledge professionals create and the ways they use them; research which is practitioner- or practice-focused; research which aims to identify the more implicit or tacit features of practice; and research which is multi-perspectival (that is, it includes the views of a variety of different players in the situation, such as service users, managers, colleagues, etc.).

A range of new and old methods and their combination might usefully serve these purposes. For instance, narrative, deconstructive or reflective methods might be used to analyse practitioner accounts of practice, and the results compared with service user perceptions of outcome to provide several different perspectives. Some of the recent social work research emerging from Finland (Karvinen, Poso and Satka 1999) very nicely illustrates the use of a range of newer methods and a commitment to researching from the practitioner's perspective (Juhila and Poso 1999; Jokinen and Suoninen 1999) and to acknowledging the difficulties in practice (Metteri 1999).

Transferability

In order to respond to the need for professional knowledge to be more flexible, the idea of transferability is useful. As discussed earlier, this involves the ability to contextualise knowledge, and thus the ability to transfer what is relevant across contexts. This involves an ability to create the knowledge about how to apply knowledge in different situations (Eraut 1994, p.54). It also involves the ability to work out which knowledge is specific to certain contexts or domains, and which is relevant elsewhere (Fook *et al.* 2000, p.245). For example, knowledge about workplace culture might be specific to a particular workplace, but knowledge about how to identify workplace culture might be transferable.

This clearly indicates several different types of research studies: a focus on the sorts of knowledge practitioners transfer between different jobs or roles is an obvious one. An examination of how practitioners use or modify knowledge across different contexts would be helpful, as well as a study of how practitioners create knowledge in the process of engaging with new situations.

Again, a mix of methods might be used, ranging from more quantitative ones which attempt to codify the types of knowledge used and the processes involved, to more inductive methods which attempt to identify ideas which are less immediately obvious.

Social contribution

It is a challenge for current professionals to both make a social contribution and remain true to their mission of service in a climate of competitive economic employment. Professional research is needed which both validates the value base of professional practice and emphasises its broader social contribution.

Much literature specific to particular professions emphasises this need. For example, in social work many writers note the imperative that research should contribute to the social justice mission of the profession (McDermott 1996; Denzin 2001). However, there might be several different directions research can take to meet these needs. For instance, the research might focus on the needs of disadvantaged or marginal groups; it might involve these groups in the research process; or it might be about professional practice with such groups. From another perspective, in order to validate the social contribution of the professions, it might be appropriate for research to focus on the sorts of social impact which professional work has made.

Last, it is imperative to research the ways in which professionals maintain and enact their values in their everyday practice. What is value-based practice and how effective is it? Does it, and if so how does it, differ from practice which is more technologically driven? What values do professionals adhere to and what strengthens them? What meaning is derived from their work and how do they see their values affecting the way they practise?

Again a variety of methods and designs are necessary. Deconstructive analyses of practice might unearth hidden values, whereas interviews and surveys might allow a clearer assessment of stated values and their impact. Evaluative measures of social impact might be relevant in tracing the broad effects of professional input.

Legitimation and accountability

On a broad level, social legitimation for professionals is about gaining and maintaining the authority and position to practise in a chosen way and to exercise influence accordingly. Current challenges involve maintaining this position for the collective good, when the push is towards breaking down such hierarchical divisions from both management and community perspectives. As I argued earlier, it is possible that moves to legitimate professional knowledge and standing do not necessarily undermine the respective positions of managers or service users or even of other colleagues. What is needed is an approach to professional knowledge which justifies its distinctive value in a number of ways, so that diverse interest groups are aware of how they can benefit from particular types of professional expertise. In other words, what professionals need to be able to do is to communicate about, or translate their expertise to, other groups like managers, community members and service users, so that they can see the benefits in their terms. This is a form of being able to 'sell' their expertise to other groups who might have different understandings of their needs.

In this way, legitimation also becomes a form of accountability, in that the process of legitimating professional expertise and knowledge to other groups is also a process of justifying the benefits to that group. Accountability and legitimation are therefore about communicating about, and ensuring the relevance of, professional expertise. In this sense, we are talking about legitimation based on accountability, rather than on pursuing social position through other structural and cultural means (e.g. through salary levels, legislation, educational level, etc.). Neither precludes the other, of course, but this perspective on legitimation indicates some strong directions for research.

With the idea of accountability being based on justification of relevance and communication of this to the diverse groups concerned, there are several major directions which professional research can take. One of the most straightforward ways in which this can be done is of course through already accepted means like collaborative (Baldwin 2000) or participative (Wadsworth 2001) approaches. Brulin (2001) notes the use of an action research approach in encouraging university research to serve community interests. Perhaps it is useful to think of these approaches and designs as also being new forms of accountability whereby ownership of and responsibility for the research are shared, and top-down relations between interest groups minimised.

However, as a general principle it is useful to be mindful of the many different ways in which research can be made more relevant – collaborative designs may not be practicable in many instances. One of the most basic starting points is simply the imperative to ensure that the reasons and motivations for the research are couched in the language and meaning system of the groups to whom it is accountable. In this sense, it is the way the material is communicated which is important, as well as the topic and substance of the research itself.

With this in mind, the research itself might become an exercise in translating the discourse of professional expertise into the discourse of managers, the discourse of other colleagues, or the thinking of service users. This idea of *research as translation exercise* (Steier 1991, p.177) is important in helping us reformulate our research directions. It indicates that we need to think of research to legitimate our professions as research which translates what we do into the language and thinking of the groups for whom and with whom we work. In this process, of course, we will find new ways to talk about, think about, and improve our work. It is also a new way of valuing and validating our work.

For instance, we might undertake some studies which aim to develop a new language for framing our practice, in terms which speak to the current debates. The professional expertise study which I undertook with my colleagues, referred to earlier in this chapter (Fook *et al.* 2000), is an example of this type of research. Research which looks at how current practice is evidence-based, and the different ways in which it is so based, would also be performing a similar function. Many studies of professional practice could contain a component of discourse analysis, providing the basis for a reframing of the discourse.

Sometimes studies might need to focus on how professional, more value-based discourse might translate into more technological frames – one need not necessarily replace the other, but studies which compared the commonalities between the two might function to facilitate better relations. Lists of competencies might prove useful, either as points of comparison, or as a basis for devising new lists. Studies might also be undertaken which compare frames of understanding between management, professional and service user groups, with a view to developing common frames of reference. In this way all views might be validated.

Workplace and inter-professional concerns

It is important that research speaks to the current concerns of the workplace in which professionals are employed. This involves economic, management, inter-organisational and inter-professional issues. While in a way I have already addressed these in broad terms, there are more specific issues concerning how professionals are legitimated and made accountable in their specific workplace which I have not discussed. For instance, given the changing nature of employment, which is less tied to pure professional qualifications, it is important that different professional groups also learn to speak a common language. Also, because of mixed funding arrangements, divisions between organisations are becoming more blurred and more complex.

Inter-professional and inter-organisational issues might be addressed through research which focuses on cross-disciplinary and organisational collaborations or teamwork. In particular, the study of how models of practice are devised which accommodate different professional cultures would provide useful data.

Since employment contracts are often more short term and more programme-specific, it is important that we understand how professional practice is grounded in, and also how it transcends, specific employment contexts. Models and documentation of best practice in these new and changing contexts would be invaluable.

Again, a variety of methods and approaches might perform such functions. Professions and organisations can be compared in any number of ways, ranging from surveys of perceptions and opinion, to the use of established instruments (such as competency lists), to interviews and observations of work, to document analysis. Best-practice models might be developed and documented using a wide variety of methods as well. For instance, journalling, focus groups or reflective methods could be used to draw out common themes or practice principles (Dadds and Hart 2001).

An approach to research for professionals:
Beyond evidence-based practice

In this chapter I have taken the view that our broad understanding of professionalism and professional practice needs to undergo review in the current context of changes. While the EBP movement is a major feature of the current context, I have argued that the broader social and global context also shapes who we are as professionals. I have tried to outline a view of how professionals, and professional research, can address challenges which are more far-reaching than the EVP debate. These challenges, of knowledge, of values and of legitimation, require research directions which support professionals in developing knowledge which is more flexible and transferable; practice which is value-based and makes a social contribution; and ways of legitimating their social position which also provide accountability.

References

Argyris, C. and Schön, D. (1974) *Theory in Practice: Increasing Professional Effectiveness.* San Francisco: Jossey Bass.

Baldwin, M. (2000) *Care Management and Community Care.* Aldershot: Ashgate.

Belenky, M., Clinchy, B., Goldberger, N. and Tarule, J. (1986) *Women's Ways of Knowing.* New York: Basic Books.

Brulin, G. (2001) 'The third task of universities or how to get universities to serve their Communities.' In P. Reason and H. Bradbury (eds) *Handbook of Action Research.* London: Sage.

Dadds, M. and Hart, S. (2001) *Doing Practitioner Research Differently.* London and New York: Routledge/Falmer.

Denzin, N. (2001) 'Social work in the seventh moment.' *Qualitative Social Work 1,* 1, 25–38.

Dominelli, L. (1996) 'Deprofessionalising social work.' *British Journal of Social Work 26,* 153–175.

Eraut, M. (1994) *Developing Professional Knowledge and Competence.* London: Falmer Press.

Fook, J. (ed.) (1996) *The Reflective Researcher: Social Workers' Experiences of Practice Research.* Sydney: Allen & Unwin.

Fook, J. (1999) 'Critical reflectivity in education and practice.' In B. Pease and J. Fook (eds) *Transforming Social Work Practice.* London: Routledge.

Fook, J. (2000) 'Deconstructing and reconstructing professional expertise.' In B. Fawcett, B. Featherstone, J. Fook and A. Rossiter (eds) *Practice and Research in Social Work.* London: Routledge.

Fook, J. (2001) 'Identifying expert social work.' In I. Shaw and N. Gould (eds) *Qualitative Research in Social Work.* London: Sage.

Fook, J. (2002) *Social Work: Critical Theory and Practice.* London: Sage.

Fook, J., Ryan, M. and Hawkins, L. (2000) *Professional Expertise: Practice, Theory and Education for Working in Uncertainty.* London: Whiting & Birch.

Friedson, E. (1970) *The Profession of Medicine.* New York: Dodd Mead.

Gibbs, A. (2001) 'The changing nature and context of social work research.' *British Journal of Social Work 31,* 687–704.

Greenwood, E. (1957) 'Attributes of a profession.' *Social Work 2,* 3, 44–55.

Gustafson, J. (1982) 'Professions as "Callings".' *Social Service Review 56,* 4, 501–515.

Hawkins, L., Ryan, M., Murray, H., Grace, M., Hawkins, G., Mendes, P. and Chatley, B. (2000) 'Supply and demand: A study of labour market trends and the employment of new social work graduates in Victoria.' *Australian Social Work 53,* 1, 35–41.

Hindmarsh, J. (1992) *Social Work Oppositions*. Aldershot: Avebury.

Hugman, R. (1991) *Power in Caring Professions*. London: Macmillan.

Ife, J. (1997) *Rethinking Social Work*. Melbourne: Longman.

Johnson, T.J. (1970) *Professions and Power*. London: Macmillan.

Jokinen, A. and Suoninen, E. (1999) 'From crime to resource: Constructing narratives in a social work encounter.' In S. Karvinen, T. Poso and M. Satka (eds) *Reconstructing Social Work Research*. Jyväskylä: University of Jyväskylä.

Juhila, K. and Poso, T. (1999) 'Local cultures in social work: Ethnographic understanding and discourse analysis in social work.' In S. Karvinen, T. Poso and M. Satka (eds) *Reconstructing Social Work Research*. Jyväskylä: University of Jyväskylä.

Karvinen, S., Poso, T. and Satka, M. (eds) (1999) *Reconstructing Social Work Research*. Jyväskylä: University of Jyväskylä.

MacDonald, C. (2000) 'The third sector in the human services: Rethinking its role.' In I. O'Connor, P. Smyth and J. Warburton (eds) *Contemporary Perspectives on Social Work and the Human Services*. Melbourne: Longman.

McDermott, F. (1996) 'Social work research: Debating the boundaries.' *Australian Social Work 49*, 1, 5–10.

Metteri, A. (1999) 'Researching difficult situations in social work.' In S. Karvinen, T. Poso and M. Satka (eds) *Reconstructing Social Work Research*. Jyväskylä: University of Jyväskylä.

Parry, N. and Parry, J. (1976) *The Rise of the Medical Profession*. London: Croom Helm.

Parton, N. (1994) 'Problematics of government, (post)modernity and social work.' *British Journal of Social Work 24*, 9–32.

Parton, N. (1998) 'Advanced liberalism, (post)modernity and social work: Some emerging social configurations.' In R.T. Meinert, J.T. Pardeck and J.W. Murphy (eds) *Postmodernity, Religion and the Future of Social Work*. New York: Haworth.

Reynolds, S. (2000) 'The anatomy of evidence-based practice.' In L. Trinder (ed.) *Evidence-based Practice*. Oxford: Blackwell.

Robertson, R. (1992) *Globalisation* London: Sage.

Rolfe, G. (2000) *Research, Truth and Authority: Postmodern Perspectives on Nursing*. London: Macmillan.

Rossiter, A. (1996) 'Finding meaning for social work in transitional times.' In N. Gould and I. Taylor (eds) *Reflective Learning for Social Work*. Aldershot: Avebury.

Scott, D. (1990) 'Practice wisdom: The neglected source of practice research.' *Social Work 35*, 6, 564–568.

Shapiro, M. (2000) 'Professions in the post-industrial labour market.' In I. O'Connor, P. Smyth and J. Warburton (eds) *Contemporary Perspectives on Social Work and the Human Services*. Melbourne: Longman.

Steier, F. (1991) *Research and Reflexivity*. London: Sage.

Trinder, L. (2000) 'Introduction: The context of evidence-based practice.' In L. Trinder (ed.) *Evidence-based Practice: A Critical Appraisal*. Oxford: Blackwell.

Wadsworth, Y. (2001) 'The mirror, the magnifying glass, the compass and the map: Participatory action research.' In P. Reason and H. Bradbury (eds) *Handbook of Action Research*. London: Sage.

CHAPTER 3

The Extremes of Child Abuse

A Macro Approach to Measuring Effective Prevention

Colin Pritchard

Introduction

James Baldwin once said, 'If you're not part of the solution, then you're part of the problem', which is a good starting point when trying to answer the question, 'Does good social work work?' I had attempted to answer this in regard to determining what had happened to families placed on the 'At Risk of Abuse' register, and despite some methodological weakness, inevitable in a retrospective study, the results were very encouraging (Pritchard 1991). Of course, the media, and therefore the politicians, are very responsive to those tragic cases which go wrong and a child dies as a result. To be fair, governments throughout the West have felt the need to respond to high-profile cases and have sought to improve child-protection services (Zunzunegui *et al.* 1997; English *et al.* 2000). This is understandable, for when one recalls specific horror stories such as those of Maria Colwell in the 1970s and Victoria Climbié in 2000, it is easy to feel despondent as another 'social work' error is trumpeted by an outraged media, looking for convenient scapegoats. Of course, such critics always have the benefit of 20-20 vision, which is the quality of perfect hindsight. Practitioners, by contrast, have always worked with only part of the information needed, within a changing context of differential pressures, which is another way of describing social work as 'flying by the seat of one's pants'. Occasionally the broadsheets would tacitly acknowledge that ours is a difficult job, but even they tended to ask sharp questions about the effectiveness of prevention.

As a practising social worker from the pre-Social-Services era, I may surprise some colleagues by asserting that, in terms of resources for child protection, we have 'never had it so good'. The lack of resources in the past might account for the fact that in the 1970s England and Wales were the fourth-highest child killers in the Western world (Pritchard 1992a). Indeed, if I have a criticism of social services it is the under-prioritisation of mental health services relative to child protection. But this leads to the question: Has the additional concentration on child protection done any good?

Certainly, as medicine's best results over the last century have shown, prevention is better than cure. But how do we show that we have prevented something if it has not happened? An answer was to build upon the classic Durkheimian thesis that changes in mortality rates reflect changes in a society, starkly seen in comparisons of infant mortality rates in, for example, Western Europe and Africa. Previous work, which incidentally was unpalatable to the government of the day, showed that internationally, as un-employment rose, so too did suicide, especially amongst young males (Pritchard 1988, 1992b, 1996). The approach was a simple measurement of death rates 'before and after'. But what has this to do with measuring effective prevention? Instead of trying to measure successful prevention, which means trying to count the number of events that did not happen – that is, proving a negative – one might measure instead the failures of the child protection services. The hardest evidence of failure to protect a child is the death of a child, which of course is exactly what the media are especially incensed about.

Of course, the majority of child neglect and abuse does not lead to a fatality, but it can be argued that it is the 'tip of the iceberg', and international research agrees that the extreme consequence of child abuse is a dead child (Kempe and Kempe 1978; De Silva and Oates 1993; Stroud 1997). Therefore, changes in children's homicide rates nationally may be seen as a macro-level indicator, for better or worse, of the effectiveness of the particular country's child-protective services (Pritchard 1992a, 1996, 2002; English *et al.* 2000).

When this approach was first used on child homicide data for the 1980s, to be honest, I was not expecting to find what I did find (Pritchard 1992a). Indeed, the results were so surprising that they attracted the widest possible criticism, with no less than three papers in the *British Journal of Social Work* from eminent researchers suggesting we had got it wrong (Creighton 1993; Lindsey and Trocme 1994; MacDonald 1995). These problems were answered (Pritchard 1993, 1996) but I am indebted to the critics' helpful comments which helped to strengthen the methodology, which has been said to have resolved the problems inherent in cross-national comparisons (Shah and De 1998), and has been used in other areas of controversial research (e.g. Pritchard 2002; Pritchard and Baldwin 2002; Pritchard and Butler 2003; Pritchard and Evans 2001).

We have known for many years, however, that child homicide rates vary across the three children's age bands of babies (aged less than one year), infants (1–4 years) and children (5–14 years) (Kempe and Kempe 1978). Babies have by some way the highest rate, infants less, and children the lowest rate in respect to the population of babies, infants and children. International studies have shown that in baby (<1 year) and infant (1–4 years) homicides the assailants are predominantly parents (Bourget and Labelle 1992; Pritchard and Bagley 2001), which means that any evaluation has to separate out these age bands, since in practice most child protection is focused upon younger children, and it is the baby and infant homicide rates which give one the best idea of how successful or not a child-protection service has been over time. This chapter takes this macro approach to exploring the effectiveness of services in England and Wales over the past 20 years or so, by examining children's homicide rates in England and Wales and the other major Western countries between 1974 and 1997.

Methodology

I appreciate that often people feel that 'methodology' is boring, but it is the one means of 'quality control' we have, which is why research published in the major journals of a discipline can be better relied upon than a quick and cheerful article in a professional magazine. Indeed, new professionals will have to face the challenges posed as internet systems become easier to use and more accessible, and the range of sources of information expands; but how are they to judge the value, reliability and validity of this information, unless by exploring how the information was collected?

A fuller explanation of the method is given elsewhere (Pritchard 2002; Pritchard and Baldwin 2002), but in brief, the procedure is as follows. The latest available international, age-related, standardised mortality statistics were taken from the World Health Organisation (WHO 1976–2000) to compare the ten major developed countries – that is, those with populations of 16 million or over. The comparisons are first based upon an *internal* comparison for each country's recorded deaths by homicide over time, in each age band – baby, infant and child – so that like is being compared with like. To determine the proportional changes in each country, ratios of change are calculated from the summed actual totals for the baseline and index years. Thus, a country is first measured against itself, and it is the ratios of change which are then used to make comparisons among the countries. This deals with the problems that would otherwise arise from variations in methods of recording homicides. A series of chi square tests were carried out to determine how the rates in England and Wales changed compared to the other countries.

Results

During the 1970s period there were 447 recorded homicides of children in England and Wales, an average of 89.4 per annum, as shown in Table 3.1. At the end of the period (1993–1997), children's homicides fell from 7.5 per month to 3.8 per month.

While baby homicide always had the highest rate of the three age bands, there was a statistically significant fall in the numbers of under-five homicides. Initially there had been 318 such deaths, compared to 129 for the older children (aged 5–14), but over the period these figures fell to 142 and 85 respectively (χ^2=5.1214,1 d/f, p<0.024). However, there were greater reductions in road deaths of children than in children's homicides, for in 1974–78, there were 6.4 children's road deaths to each homicide, and by 1993–97 this ratio was 4.5 to one.

Table 3.1a Actual numbers of children's homicide and road deaths, England and Wales, 1974–78 to 1993–97

Year	Baby	Infant	Child	Total
1974	35	40	31	106
1975	35	30	23	86
1976	36	26	23	85
1977	18	33	27	78
1978	29	38	25	92
Total 1974–78	151	167	129	447
1993	20	28	11	59
1994	13	19	15	47
1995	8	11	24	43
1996	13	14	23	50
1997	8	8	12	28
Total 1993–97	62	80	85	227

Table 3.1b Rates per million of children's homicide and road deaths, England and Wales, 1974–78 to 1993–97

Year	Baby	Infant	Child	Total
1974	55	14	4	73
1975	55	11	3	69
1976	62	10	3	75
1977	32	13	3	48
1978	49	16	3	68
Average 1974–78	51	13	3.2	67
1993	30	10	2	42
1994	20	7	2	29
1995	12	4	4	20
1996	20	5	4	29
1997	12	3	2	17
Average 1993–97	19	6	2.8	27
Ratio of change	0.37	0.46	0.88	0.40

Table 3.2 Five-year children's homicide deaths, 1974–78 to 1993–97: Summed actual numbers and index of change

Country and Year	Baby	Infant	Child	Homicides
Australia				
1970s	45	33	66	144
1990s	34	55	59	148
Index	0.76	1.67	0.89	1.03
Canada				
1970s	22	44	48	114
1990s	61	65	83	209
Index	2.77	1.48	1.73	1.83
England and Wales				
1970s	151	167	129	447
1990s	62	80	85	227
Index	0.42	0.48	0.66	0.51
France				
1970s	79	96	124	299
1990s	96	75	122	293
Index	1.22	0.78	0.98	0.98
*Germany**				
1970s	275	246	366	887
1990s	111	129	166	406
Index	0.40	0.52	0.45	0.46
Italy				
1970s	29	32	109	170
1990s	16	30	52	98
Index	0.55	0.94	0.48	0.58
Japan				
1970s	839	986	867	2692
1990s	189	214	204	607
Index	0.23	0.22	0.24	0.23
Netherlands				
1970s	20	18	30	68
1990s	18	14	34	66
Index	0.90	0.78	1.13	0.97

Continued on next page…

... *Table 3.2 continued*

Country and Year	Baby	Infant	Child	Homicides
Spain				
1970s	19	14	43	76
1990s	12	10	19	41
Index	0.63	0.71	0.44	0.54
USA				
1970s	852	1562	2066	4480
1990s	1617	2184	2755	6556
Index	1.90	1.40	1.33	1.46

*Germany's figure for the 1970s includes the DDR

Table 3.2 shows the numbers of children's homicide deaths in each age band over the period for England and Wales, the USA and the other countries.

To allow for differences in population rates, Table 3.3 gives the baby and total children's homicide summed rates per million, in descending order of the extent of reductions in children's homicide over the period.

Four countries had substantial falls (a change ratio of <0.80) in children's homicide over the period, namely Japan (0.35), England and Wales (0.41), Germany (0.56) and the Netherlands (0.58). On the other hand, there were substantial rises in the USA, from 446 to 622 per million (ratio 1.40) and in France, where the comparable figure rose from 112 to 177 (ratio 1.58).

In regard to children's homicide, the reduction in England and Wales was statistically greater than in any other country, with the exception of Japan.

England and Wales thus did considerably better than the USA in terms of a reduced rate of homicide of children, while compared with the European countries which also saw substantial falls in children's homicide (Germany and the Netherlands), the England and Wales reductions were greater to a statistically significant degree (p <0.03 and p <0.02 respectively).

Table 3.3 Children's homicide deaths 1974–78 to 1993–97: Summed rates per million per age band and index of change

Country and Year	Baby	Homicides
Japan		
1974–78	91	126
1993–97	32	44
Index	0.35	0.35
England and Wales		
1974–78	51	67
1993–97	19	27
Index	0.51	0.40
*Germany**		
1974–78	53	69
1993–97	27	39
Index	0.58	0.57
Netherlands		
1974–78	38	50
1993–97	22	29
Index	0.58	0.58
Australia		
1974–78	35	50
1991–95	27	43
Index	0.77	0.86
Canada		
1974–78	30	50
1993–97	32	46
Index	1.00	1.10
Italy		
1974–78	7	10
1991–95	7	11
Index	1.00	1.10
Spain		
1974–78	5	8
1991–95	6	9
Index	1.2	1.13

Continued on next page...

...*Table 3.3 continued*

Country and Year	Baby	Homicides
USA		
1974–78	53	89
1993–97	81	124
Index	1.53	1.39
France		
1974–78	15	22
1992–96	26	35
Index	1.73	1.59

*Germany's figure for the 1970s includes the DDR.

Discussion

Whenever mortality rates change, it is important to establish whether this is an artefact of changes in something other than the real rate of homicide. For example, willingness to record the death of a child as a homicide may change over time (English *et al.* 2000), but it seems unlikely that this could account for the changes found in the period under review, since the process by which states established reliable, rational systems for recording deaths and detecting homicides was completed earlier in the twentieth century. Hence, for example, the unexpected rises in the USA rates are unlikely to be an artefact. Consequently, these results can be seen as reasonably reliable *indicators* of real changes which occurred in children's road and homicide deaths over the period.

Table 3.4 England and Wales – Total children's homicides compared with other major countries, 1974/1997: Chi square results

Country	Road	Homicide
(England & Wales v.)	chi square	chi square
USA	12.5757 < 0.0003	103.1449 < 0.0000
Australia	4.0186 < 0.05	28.1316 < 0.0000
Canada	0.7868 n.sig	35.1843 < 0.0000
France	17.0847 < 0.0001	76.6922 < 0.0000
Germany	1.9079 n.sig	5.0373 < 0.03
Italy	3.9693 < 0.05	19.3437 < 0.0000
Japan	0.3171 n.sig	1.7269 n.sig
Netherlands	4.7561 < 0.03	5.8053 < 0.02
Spain	26.9641 < 0.0000	17.7349 < 0.0000

The findings can be summarised as follows. Baby homicide is predominantly linked to intra-family child abuse (De Silva and Oates 1993); it is within their birth families that the risk to babies is found. Four countries showed significant children's homicide reductions, but England and Wales did significantly better than all other countries except Japan. This reflects well on child protection services, as during the period England and Wales had one of the worst relative child poverty rates in the European Union (Policy Action Team 2000), and the child protection services in England and Wales therefore had relatively severe problems to cope with over the period. There were unexpected rises in children's homicide in France and in the USA. One explanatory factor for the USA may be the availability of guns in North American households (De Cherney 1999); but since the USA has always had more weapons in circulation than Western European countries, thus explaining the USA's *higher* rate, it does not explain the reasons for the *increase* in children's homicide during a period in which the adult homicide rate in the USA declined (Pritchard and Evans 2001).

Conclusions

There are no grounds for complacency in England and Wales, since nearly four children a month were homicide victims. Nonetheless, this figure is far exceeded by the numbers of road deaths, and in terms of the media cries of 'How safe are our children?', the average British child is far more at risk (22 times more at risk) from us and our fellow-motorists than from the homicidal strangers of our nightmares. As the majority of children's homicides occur within families who are often psychosocially and psychiatrically disturbed (De Silva and Oates 1993; Pritchard and Bagley 2001), it would appear that there is one child homicide per month where the child is from an 'average' family, and the killing is perpetrated by an external assailant (Pritchard and Bagley 2001). This is still an unacceptable rate, but, to reiterate, it is far short of the numbers of children killed on the roads in England and Wales.

What about the international picture? We cannot explain the substantial rises in child homicides in France; to do so will require a country-specific research project. However, we can make a brief comment about the USA results, since after all it was the USA that first alerted and taught the world about the extremes of child neglect and abuse (Kempe *et al.* 1962; English *et al.* 2000). Alan Butler and I have looked specifically at the USA child-homicide situation (Pritchard and Butler 2003) and were startled to find that, within a falling adult homicide rate, their children's homicides had risen considerably. We know that the USA violent-mortality situation compared to the rest of the Western world is badly skewed because of the prevalence of easy access to weapons. Indeed, it was found that there were more youth and young adult homicide victims in the USA than there were fatal American casualties in the Vietnam war (Pritchard and Evans 2001), but guns have always been available and this cannot account for the rises. However, there is evidence that during the Reagan and the first Bush presidencies, there were major reductions in a range of welfare provisions, with the inevitable effects of a worsening economic situation and increased child neglect (Gilham *et al.* 1998; Mishra 1999). It has been shown that there are direct links between resource expenditure and outcome, for example in cancer care (Evans and Pritchard 2000), and, despite the pressures, social services in England and Wales have been relatively successful in hanging on to their child protection budgets. In contrast, the situation in the USA is truly fraught: while in the USA as elsewhere the research shows that, in terms of numbers, we motorists are more fatal to children than external assailants (Pritchard 2002), over the past five years the USA on average had 1200 children's homicides and 2600 children's road deaths, a very different ratio from that found in Britain. We can conclude that there are serious problems with the child protection system in the USA compared to that in England and Wales. Certainly, I am not complacent. Indeed, in view of what is known about the child-protection–psychiatric interface and child homicide (Pritchard and Bagley 2001), we might do even better if we further improved the collaboration between the two – hence my earlier criticisms at the relative decline in social services mental-health provision.

Finally, these results might go some way towards reassuring the public that the child protection services in England and Wales are amongst the best in the developed world, as we fell from being high in the 'league table' of baby killers in the 1970s, to being fourth lowest. Nonetheless, the outrage about a murdered child is totally understandable (Laming 2001). Moreover, despite the major reductions in our children's homicides, these fatalities represent but the tip of the iceberg of suffering, as they give no indication of the numbers of children who are severely disabled and injured by their experience of neglect and abuse.

While there is no case for reducing the child protection services, a better informed public might wish to pay greater attention to reducing the toll of children's deaths on the roads. Furthermore, perhaps the media might give a belated acknowledgement of the achievements of the child protection services in England and Wales?

References

Bourget, D. and Labelle, A. (1992) 'Homicide, infanticide and filicide.' *Clinical Forensic Psychiatry 15*, 661–673.

Creighton, S. (1993) 'Children's homicide: An exchange.' *British Journal of Social Work 23*, 6, 634–644.

De Cherney, G.S. (1999) 'Gun control as a public health issue.' *Delaware Medical Journal 23*, 229–233.

De Silva, S. and Oates, R.K. (1993) 'Child homicide – The extreme of child abuse.' *Medical Journal of Australia 134*, 560–571.

English, D.J., Wingard, T., Marshall, D., Orme, M. and Orme, A. (2000) 'Alternative responses to child protection services: Emerging issues and concerns.' *Child Abuse and Neglect 24*, 3, 375–388.

Evans, B.T. and Pritchard, C. (2000) 'Cancer survival rates and GDP expenditure on health. A comparison of England & Wales and the USA.' *Public Health 114*, 336–339.

Gilham, B., Tanner, G. and Cheyne, B. (1998) 'Unemployment rates, single parent density and indices of child poverty. Their relationship to different categories of child abuse.' *Child Abuse and Neglect 22*, 2, 79–90.

Kempe, C.H., Silverman, F.N., Steele, B.F., Draegmuller, W. and Silver, H.K. (1962) 'The battered child syndrome.' *Journal of the American Medical Association 181*, 17–24.)

Kempe, H. and Kempe, C.H. (1978) *Child Abuse*. Chicago: University of Chicago Press.

Laming, Lord (2001) *Chair's Opening Statement to the Victoria Climbié*. London: Department of Health (www.victoria-climbie-inquiry.org.uk).

Lindsey, M.J. and Trocme, N. (1994) 'Have child protection efforts reduced child homicides? An examination of data from Britain and North America.' *British Journal of Social Work 24*, 6, 715–732.

MacDonald, K. (1995) 'Comparative homicide and the proper aims of social work. A sceptical note.' *British Journal of Social Work 25*, 4, 489–498.

Mishra, R. (1999) *Globalization and the Welfare State*. Cheltenham: Edward Elgar.

Policy Action Team (2000) *National Strategy for Neighbourhood Renewal: Report 12: Young People*. London: The Stationery Office.

Pritchard, C. (1988) 'Suicide, gender and unemployment in the British Isles and the EEC, 1974–85.' *Social Psychiatry and Psychiatric Epidemiology 23*, 85–89.

Pritchard, C. (1991) 'Levels of risk and psychosocial problems in families on the "At Risk of Abuse Register": Some indices of outcome two years after case closure.' *Research Policy and Planning 9*, 1, 12–26.

Pritchard, C. (1992a) 'Children's homicide as an indicator of effective child protection. A comparative study of European statistics.' *British Journal of Social Work 22*, 6, 663–684.

Pritchard, C. (1992b) 'Is there a link between suicide in young men and unemployment? A UK comparison with other EEC countries.' *British Journal of Psychiatry 160*, 750–756.

Pritchard, C. (1996) 'Search for an indicator of effective child protection in a re-analysis of child homicide in the major Western World countries 1973–1992. A response to Lindsey and Trocme, and McDonald.' *British Journal of Social Work 26*, 4, 545–564.

Pritchard, C. (2002) 'Children's homicide and road deaths in England & Wales and the USA: An international comparison 1974–1997.' *British Journal of Social Work 32*, 4, 495–502.

Pritchard, C. and Bagley, C. (2001) 'A decade of child homicide assailants and their suicide, and suicide in a two-year cohort of child sex abusers.' *Journal of Forensic Psychiatry 12*, 273–290.

Pritchard, C. and Baldwin, D.S. (2002) 'Elderly suicides in Asian and English-speaking countries.' *Acta Psychiatrica Scandinavica 105*, 1–5.

Pritchard, C. and Butler, A.J. (2003) 'Child homicide in the USA and the western world 1974–97: A cause for concern?' *Journal of Family Violence*, in press.

Pritchard, C. and Evans, B.T. (2001) 'An international comparison of "Youth" (15–24) and "Young Adult" (25–34) homicide in the USA and western world 1974–94: The USA anomaly.' *Critical Public Health 11*, 83–93.

Shah, A. and De, T. (1998) 'Suicide and the elderly: A review.' *International Journal of Psychiatry in Clinical Practice 2*, 3–17.

Stroud, J. (1997) 'Mental disorder and the homicide of children: A review.' *Social Work and Social Sciences Review 6*, 149–162.

WHO (1976–2000) *World Health Statistics Annual Review*, 31–36 (Table 1 accessible at www.who.int.whois).

Zunzunegui, M.V., Morales, J.M. and Martinez, V. (1997) 'Child abuse: Socio-economic factors and health status.' *Annuals Espania Pediatrica 47*, 33–41.

CHAPTER 4

Effective Social Work

A Micro Approach – Reducing Truancy, Delinquency and School Exclusions

Colin Pritchard

Introduction

It is appreciated that statistics, especially morbidity statistics, can be a real turn-off, and my own chapter on child homicide in this volume might, despite its inherently encouraging message, appear gloomy. Moreover, a 'macro' approach, based on national data, reflects the weakness inherent in all aggregated data: it tells us nothing about the individual. To offset that social policy 'big picture', let us turn to a project which was primarily geared to the front-line social worker, which is a good 'micro' example demonstrating that good social work works.

Social work has always been 'political' in the sense that how society deals with its 'social ills' reflects the philosophical positions which underpin the major parties' positions (Pritchard and Taylor 1978). Thus, the debate about how to reduce youth crime (Home Office 1997a, 1997b; Boateng 2000) involves a particular understanding of the 'causes of crime' and whether preventative, or deterrent and punitive, measures are best (Audit Commission 1998; Goldblatt and Lewis 1998). Morally, few can quarrel with the need for evidence of effective intervention, especially in measures to prevent child and family dysfunctional behaviour and the concomitant truancy, delinquency and educational under-achievement. Such problems are associated with a range of psychosocial 'pathologies' (Audit Commission

1998; Rutter *et al.* 1998), seen in the convergence of criminological, child psychiatric and psychological research, which indicates that crime, mental disorder and child neglect often have common roots (Akehurst *et al.* 1995; Audit Commission 1996, 1998; Farrington 1995; Rutter *et al.* 1998; Pritchard *et al.* 1992a, 1992b, 1997; Pritchard and Cox 1997). Hence, this chapter describes a front-line, school-based social work service that sought to break into this 'cycle'of psychosocial deprivation.

We do not need to rehearse here the well-established research which indicates the importance of the interaction of individuals with their family and within their community for understanding these problems, and the particular importance of socio-economic deprivation (Farrington 1995; Graham and Bowling 1995; Audit Commission 1996; Social Exclusion Unit 1998; Lyon *et al.* 2000; Boateng 2000). Nonetheless, we would agree with Rutter that it is the quality of intra-family relationships that is the most important mediator (Rutter and Smith 1995).

The value of placing a social work service in school is that the school is a 'normative' institution, universal and at the heart of any community (O'Keefe 1994; Blyth and Milner 1998; Dupper 1998; Social Exclusion Unit 1998); as Farrington (1995) says, 'poverty, low intelligence and early school failure lead to truancy and lack of educational qualifications, which in turn leads to low status jobs and periods of unemployment', all of which 'make it harder to achieve goals legitimately', a neat description of the cycle of deprivation.

The project

The initiative discussed here emerged from previously separate research projects, which the Chief Officers of the county, in education, health, probation and social services, recognised were relevant to all aspects of their work. It attracted major Home Office funding and the full report can be obtained, free of charge, from the Home Office website (Pritchard 2001). The study was a three-year project to provide a school-based child and family social work service, in linked primary and secondary schools, that was contrasted against two matched schools for purposes of comparison. All four schools drew their children from the county's most socio-economically disadvantaged areas. Indeed the estate upon which the project primary school was based, 'Attlee' (all names are pseudonyms), had proportionately the highest rate of families with children on the 'At Risk of Abuse' register in the county. Moreover, as the county still had the 11-plus examination, neither secondary school had the full spread of academic ability, as they were close to two local selective grammar schools.

The project aimed to:

1. assist children and families to maximise their educational and social opportunities

2. facilitate teachers' role in educating and socialising the child in the school

3. enhance community–school and other agency collaboration

4. reduce truancy and criminality

5. reduce exclusion from school.

These were tough and demanding objectives indeed, and all with measurable outcomes.

The project was led by a senior educational social worker from a service whose social work staff were all qualified. The primary school had a full-time teacher-counsellor, and the secondary school a part-time teacher-counsellor. They could either assist in the classroom to deal with educational difficulties, or be available to respond to child, family or classroom crises. This provided the classroom teacher with a range of alternative options, thus giving the child the individual attention they required, while minimising any potential disruption for the rest of the class. The school's pastoral tutors routinely referred any children who demonstrated distress or disturbance. Moreover, if the educational social worker (ESW) was not immediately available, they could respond themselves to parents, and thus to the child; the classroom teacher and the family were able to obtain virtually an immediate response to their difficulty.

The project leader's role was first to provide parental support, helping to reduce any family disturbance which might impact upon the child's ability to benefit from their education. This involved counselling, practical advice and often being an advocate with other agencies on behalf of the school's families. Parents valued the ease of access and a continuity of assistance, which was in contrast to their usual experience of only crisis help. The team leader offered long-term support, and the team could provide drop-in advice, which often helped to head off potential problems. As one headteacher put it: 'When the project began they were fire-fighting, later they helped to stop the crises becoming emergencies, and, at the end, started dealing with the crises before they became crises.'

The ESW took referrals from parents and school staff, making special efforts to be available to all, from caretaker to headteacher. The ESW also provided an individual counselling service for the children. Truancy was seen as a serious indicator of psycho-socio-educational disturbance, and both child and parent were speedily made aware of any emerging problem. The second most important aspect of the ESW's role was offering a consultative service to teachers about their concerns about troubled or troublesome children. At the beginning of the project the ESW invited staff to choose the ten 'most time-consuming children' for referral. This quickly demonstrated to both schools the value of the team, and of maintaining the problem youngster within mainstream education, while at the same time freeing up the teacher to provide a wider professional response to the rest of the class.

Knowledge of child protection issues and procedures was essential, especially in Attlee. The project team saw their role as *supporting* the local child protection team. They quickly were seen as a resource, which often led to joint practice, which in turn furthered schools' interaction and collaboration with other agencies. The social work practitioners adopted an integrated approach, including individual counselling for child and family; group work, especially for dealing with bullying and preparation for transfer from primary to secondary schools; and community development. Crucially, the ESW had more time to develop in-depth collaboration with other services, thus enhancing external agencies' contribution to the children and families of Attlee and Bevan schools (Bevan was the secondary school to which Attlee pupils generally progressed). Thus the team provided speedy, acceptable and easy access to a child and family social work service, described by the project leader as 'optimal social work practice'.

The project ESW worked to two schools, with an average of 960 enrolled pupils, unlike the 'standard' ESW provision, where an ESW might have a population of almost 4000 pupils as a potential caseload without the support of teacher-social-workers. Moreover, the project ESW worked within a well-defined community area, maximising his time in respect to travel, liaison and collaboration with other agencies. While he had good professional supervisory support from the ESW service, he worked directly to the headteachers, and had minimal administrative responsibility to his county service. As the project developed, the team felt they had virtually an ideal professional situation. The project became a catalyst, helping staff to maximise their contribution. As one headteacher put it, 'They created a virtuous circle – as accumulatively, the positives built up, helping to improve the school's educational and community contribution.'

Two brief examples will illuminate the opportunities the 'enhanced' situation provided.

1. A mother was admitted on a compulsory basis to a psychiatric hospital, but no thought had been given to the children. The elder child, arriving late in Bevan school, was recognised as being distressed and was seen by the teacher-counsellor, who immediately alerted the ESW. By early afternoon, the ESW had visited the home, arranged alternative child-care, and liaised with the social services department, which approved the arrangements. Thus, by the end of the school day, the children's needs were catered for, avoiding any temporary care, keeping the children within their own schools, and minimising the disruption caused by the mother's admission to hospital. It was important too that the ESW could give discreet support over the next two years, helping to reduce any family stress.

2. From a 'drop-in' parent, the ESW learned about possible 'sexual grooming' behaviour by men visiting the estate. Co-operative enquiries with the community constable exposed a paedophile ring before it had a chance to develop, avoiding distress to potential victims and the local scandal which so often surrounds such incidents.

Research methodology

A range of psycho-socio-educational outcomes were compared with those in matched schools, which received only the 'standard' educational social work provision, i.e. one ESW for between six and eight schools. A fuller description of the methodology can be found elsewhere (Pritchard 2001; Pritchard and Williams 2001).

The project primary school was designated 'Attlee' and was on the second most socio-economically disadvantaged estate in the county. Attlee was a feeder school for the project's secondary school, 'Bevan'. They were matched against comparative schools, the primary school 'Churchill' and the secondary school 'Disraeli', for which Churchill was the feeder. The evaluation consisted of a multi-methodological, quasi-experimental comparative approach. This included ten different, complementary studies. Access to the police, probation, education and social services allowed the project's work to be placed in the context of local services.

A range of change outcomes from year 1 to year 3 of the project were selected for measurement and evaluation. These included the project's first year of counselling, a consumer survey with children and parents, teachers' stress levels before and after the project (Borg *et al.* 1991), and teachers' views of the project. Crucially, annual measurements were taken of the attitudes and behaviour of the four schools' pupils (n = 2000) via a confidential, self-administered questionnaire. Finally, exclusion rates and GCSE examination results were monitored over the period of the project, and a cost–benefit analysis was undertaken to estimate the 'value added' (Morgan and Murgatroyd 1994), based upon Home Office costings of an offence (Coopers and Lybrand 1994), and education costs for excluded children. No hard data were available for costs to the social services department or to health services, so these were not included in the cost–benefit analysis. Savings are therefore underestimated.

Differences between the schools were tested by the chi square test, but to examine changes over time a ratio of ratios (ROR) was calculated. An example best illustrates the use of ROR. In the first year of the project, Bevan school had 41 per cent girls and 59 per cent boy pupils, a ratio of 1.44:1 boys to girls. By the third year, as a result of changes in other school intakes, it was 36 per cent to 64 per cent, a boy:girl ratio of 1.78:1. To obtain a ratio of change, divide the current by the previous ratio, which gives 1.24. Hence, proportionately, there were 24 per cent more boys in Bevan than at the start of the project. Disraeli school in the first year had 45 per cent girls and 55 per cent boys, a ratio of 1.22:1. This became 47 per cent and 53 per cent in the third year, a ratio of 1.12:1. This gives a ratio of change of 0.92 – that is, there were proportionately fewer boys in Disraeli than previously. To calculate the ratio of ratios (ROR) divide one ratio of change by the other, i.e. 1.24 by 0.92, which yields an ROR of 1.35. This means that, compared to Disraeli, the numbers of male pupils rose substantially in Bevan over the period. As males continue to be more delinquent than females (Rutter and Smith 1995), this is an important factor when comparing the two secondary schools in the third year of the project.

The most important weakness was that the study could not be blind or randomised. Second, the evaluation had to focus upon broad outcome measures, rather than individual child/family situations, as there was only one part-time researcher, which constrained the potential range for in-depth analysis.

The context

Unemployment

Unemployment in the project's region was especially affected by the recession of the mid-1990s, and proportionately had the third biggest rise in unemployment in the UK (Department of Employment 1992–1997). All schools in the study were in areas with higher unemployment rates than the regional average. Churchill, the comparative primary school, had double the regional unemployment rate, but Attlee had almost four times the regional jobless level, averaging 42 per cent over three years, while Bevan and Disraeli schools had almost treble the regional out-of-work level. Thus project families and their communities experienced unprecedented increases in joblessness, as well as a sharp reduction in available jobs – contextual factors likely to exacerbate any family or community tensions over the period.

Statutory service contact

At the beginning of the project, 11 per cent of families of children at Attlee school were in formal contact with either probation or social services departments; at the end this had fallen to 5.6 per cent of families. This was in sharp contrast to the control primary school, Churchill, whose initial contact rate was 2.1 per cent, but rose to 3.7 per cent of families by year 3. The rate for the project secondary school Bevan went from 1.7 per cent to 4.3 per cent, and for the comparator school Disraeli it went from 2.25 per cent to 3.9 per cent by the final year. Thus, whilst Attlee families were still more likely by the end of the project to be in contact with statutory agencies, the apparent need for this content reduced to a statistically significant extent during the time of the project.

Crime on the estate

The estate served by Attlee school had an adult male criminality rate of 24 per cent compared to the county average of 6 per cent (measured by the proportion of adult males with a conviction for an indictable offence). However, household victimisation on the estate fell from 11 per cent of households a year to 7.4 per cent during the project. Attlee adult offenders had been convicted of an average of nine indictable crimes each, reminding us that 6 per cent of offenders are responsible for almost two-thirds of all crime (Home Office 1998). It is not clear that the fall in local victimisation can be attributed to the project's influence on community development, but it is still an encouraging indication.

Intergenerational problems

A study of 228 former Attlee pupils, now aged 22–27, found that 8.7 per cent of the men and 10.2 per cent of the women were currently known to the social services department. This was nine times the age-related county average. Furthermore, the young women had five times the age-related pregnancy rate of the rest of the county.

An in-depth analysis of 36 case records from the Attlee family social services department showed that two-fifths had child-protection problems; more than one in ten had mental health difficulties; and one in five had medical and chronic disorders. Both sub-studies highlight the intergenerational nature of many of the children's families.

Contextually, the children in all four schools, but especially those from the Attlee estate, belonged to far more disadvantaged backgrounds than the county average.

Project outcomes

Psychosocial outcomes

In the first year Attlee had proportionately the highest child protection referrals in the county, but this fell by 76 per cent by the third year. This coincided with a 30 per cent rise in child protection referrals from the other estates linked to the 'comparative' schools and the rest of the county, yielding an ROR of 3.70. Such a change appears indicative of improvements in the cohesiveness of families in the project area.

Child and family counselling

In the first year the team dealt with 94 cases, which were assessed weekly. Most cases were multi-problem but the main presenting difficulties were behavioural disorders (54%), 'neurotic/anxiety' difficulties (29%) and reactive educational problems (11%). In 9 per cent of cases medical problems were contributing to the child's maladjustment, and in 18 per cent the problems were assessed as the parents' rather than the child's. Most referrals were from the school, but 10 per cent were extra-school referrals and 9 per cent and 22 per cent were child and parental self-referrals, respectively. The outcomes were that 40 per cent of the problems were assessed as totally resolved, 46 per cent as much improved, 9 per cent as improved, 2 per cent as unchanged, and 3 per cent as having become worse or much worse.

Consumers' views: Children's and families' questionnaire

Children's and their parents' views were sought on how helpful/unhelpful their social worker was. This separate countywide consumer study of the Educational Social Work Service has been reported in detail elsewhere (Pritchard *et al.* 1998), but suffice it to say here that the project social worker was significantly more valued by families than the average, standard service educational social worker. Key findings were that clients felt individualised; valued the easy and acceptable availability of the project service; and, crucially, appreciated the time devoted to complex family situations.

Consumers' views: Teachers' questionnaire

Teachers' morale was assessed before and after the project in a self-report questionnaire. In year 1, the response rate was 73 per cent (n = 74) and in year 3 the response rate was 80 per cent (n = 84). In year 1 there were no significant differences between project and comparative teachers; generally they were very experienced people, the majority aged over 40, and 18 per cent had been in their current school for 11 or more years. Initially there were no significant differences between the teachers' stress levels but, by year 3, statistically significant differences had emerged, as shown in Table 4.1, as the project teachers reported far less stress than their colleagues did. An ROR of 5.52 indicated the substantial improvements in the project schoolteachers' morale.

A few structured comments exemplify how highly the 39 project schoolteachers valued the project. Excluding the 'unsure' responses, 79 per cent agreed that the project 'enhanced the pupils' integration in the school', against 3 per cent who did not. Similar proportions agreed that the project had 'contributed to improving the children's school attendance' and disagreed the project was 'a waste of time', that it 'encouraged feckless parents', or was 'irrelevant to the work of the school'. Of direct practice relevance, 92 per cent agreed (and no-one disagreed) that the project was 'supportive to staff in difficult situations'; 62 per cent (no-one disagreeing) thought that it was 'a benefit to pupils' parents'; 64 per cent against 0 per cent said that it had 'helped stop a crisis becoming an emergency'; and 79 per cent against 0 per cent found the 'accessibility of the social worker especially valuable'. Despite budget pressures, 69 per cent to 0 per cent agreed that it 'should have priority for future funding'. Hence, from the teachers' perspective, the project was largely successful in its aim of enhancing the children's identification with school.

	Year 1 project n=34 (%)	Year 1 comparative n=40 (%)	Year 3 project n=39 (%)	Year 3 comparative n=45 (%)
Same stress as others	62	55	74	69
More stress than others	29	35	3	20
Less or have no stress at work	9	10	23	11

Table 4.1 Teachers' stress, years 1 and 3

There were in-depth interviews with a 25 per cent sample of project school-teachers and the two headteachers. Space precludes full reporting of the results here, but one respondent, who had been overtly hostile to the project, said: 'I belong to a very traditional approach to teaching, and I do not care who knows it.' But he also said: 'I'm happy that the project is here because it helped the children, and got feckless parents off my back so I could do the job I should be doing, teaching the children.' With such a 'critic', readers can imagine the enthusiastic responses of the majority of teachers, epitomised in the primary's head's comment: 'When the project first started it was fire-fighting – then stopped the crises becoming emergencies, and in the last year, it began to head off the crises.' The secondary school's satisfaction was shown when the governors independently incorporated the social-work post into the school's establishment.

One issue emerging from the interviews was the extent to which the project staff, especially the social worker, were 'exceptional'. Could another group of staff, appropriately trained and orientated, take their place? Most respondents had little doubt that despite the excellence of the team, it was the principle of the initiative, rather than the individuals involved, which was effective.

Project and control school pupil questionnaires (years 1–3)

It was hypothesised that social work with client children and families would accumulatively benefit the rest of the school; as class situations became less difficult, the children would be better able to realise their educational and social opportunities. In turn, teachers would have more time and energy to serve both the 'clients' of the project and the rest of the class. Thus it was hypothesised that there should be measurable improvements in all the project children. Annual surveys enabled us to contrast any changes between the project and comparative schools.

PRIMARY SCHOOLS, YEARS 1–3

Children aged nine or over in the schools completed the anonymous self-administered questionnaire. The socio-economic disadvantage of the schools, especially Attlee, is seen in the simple fact that, over the three years, 45 per cent of Attlee compared to 18 per cent of Churchill children received free school dinners.

In respect of problematic behaviour, key improvements were found in respect to theft. Initially Attlee had a far worse self-reported rate of theft (63% against 26%), but by year 3, Attlee's rate fell to a similar level to Churchill's, and the marked improvement was seen in an ROR of 2.71. Other improvements related both to a decline in 'frequent fighting' at Attlee, 48 per cent to 29 per cent, with an ROR of 1.66 showing Attlee improving over time, and to a fall in the rate of bullying, down to 17 per cent, with an ROR of 1.12. However, there was a big gap between children's perception of bullying as a serious problem and their own experience of being bullied. This divergence probably reflects the anxiety of children about bullying. All delinquent behaviour, be it truancy or stealing, occurred more often in the company of other children, indicating the influence of peers and justifying the extra effort given by the project to developing group activity, particularly in respect to bullying.

IDENTIFICATION WITH THE SCHOOL

Pupils were asked what they thought was important for schools to teach from a range of topics, for example 'learning right from wrong', 'avoiding trouble in class', 'getting on with others', the '3 Rs' and 'getting a good job'. Initially Churchill children scored significantly higher on all statements. By year 3, however, Attlee's pupils had a slightly better response than Churchill's, and of particular importance was how Attlee had increased its 'enjoy school' rating compared with Churchill over the three years: 54–75 per cent to 69–72 per cent, an ROR of 1.33.

SECONDARY SCHOOLS, YEARS 1–3

Both Bevan and Disraeli schools increased the numbers of pupils during the three years of the project, following reorganisation in other schools. One consequence was that, by year 3, Bevan school had more 14–16-year-old boys (65% compared with 53% in Disraeli). By year 3, the rate of unemployed fathers in the schools was respectively 2.5 and 2.8 times the regional jobless level, while more than a third of pupils belonged to a single-parent family.

PROBLEMATIC BEHAVIOUR

Table 4.2 shows the changing pattern of problematic behaviour.

In relation to theft, Bevan's pupils had significantly less problematic behaviour than Disraeli's did. Furthermore, they generally had positive RORs, indicating that relative to the schools' initial levels of delinquent behaviour, Bevan's improved over the period in comparison both to Disraeli and to its own base rate, showing in particular a much lower level of theft from school. Truancy and frequent truancy fell dramatically, while the reduction in frequent fighting in Bevan school, like the much lower theft from school, reflected improved relationships within the project school. Vandalism worsened in Disraeli, whilst Bevan's repair bills in year 3 were the lowest they had been for five years. There were improvements in Bevan pupils' solvent and substance misuse, whose initial profile had been worse than Disraeli's. Of particular significance was the marked fall in frequent misuse of hard drugs by the Bevan students. In parenthesis, all children involved in drug and solvent misuse were also involved in smoking tobacco, emphasising the importance of the use of tobacco as an introduction to serious drug misuse (Mindle 1995).

Table 4.2 Problematic behaviour, Bevan and Disraeli schools, 14–16-year-olds

Problems	Bevan year 1 n=272 (%)	Bevan year 3 n=356 (%)	Disraeli year 1 n=365 (%)	Disraeli year 3 n=503 (%)	Ratio of ratios, years 1 –3
Truancy	28	16	40	37 ***	1.62
Truants often	12	11	22	31 ***	1.54
Fights often	22	20	26	29 *	1.23
Vandalises	28	28	37	44 **	1.19
Bullying perception	17	29	29	44 **	0.89
Been bullied	13	10	14	12	1.11
All theft	21	23	41	49 ***	1.09
Underage drinking	24	22	28	35 *	1.36
Solvents	18 *	5	8	9 *	4.05
Cannabis	18	26	19	27	0.98
Hard drugs	11 *	10	7	12	1.89
Hard drugs often	7 *	4	3	9 **	5.25

***$P<0.001$ **$P<0.01$ *$P<0.05$.

In respect to under-age drinking, Bevan had a slightly better record than Disraeli, 22 to 35 per cent, with an ROR of 1.21. However, this may be one of the few 'negative' gender items, since Disraeli school, having more girls, is likely to have had more potential under-aged drinkers, as girls are more easily accepted by publicans than under-aged boys. Changes in the *perception* of bullying was an area in which Bevan did relatively less well than Disraeli, with an ROR of 0.89 for Bevan. This may be because students felt less safe, or because there were more boys in Bevan, or, paradoxically, because the influence of the project in raising the issue of bullying may have increased awareness of the topic and heightened the perception of bullying as a problem. The influence of peers can not be overstated, as *all* problematic behaviour by the secondary school students, especially drug-taking, occurred more often in groups than alone.

ATTITUDES TO SCHOOL

Initially there was little difference in views of what schools should teach. After three years, however, Bevan pupils' attitudes were significantly more positive than Disraeli's. For example, 80 per cent of Bevan pupils agreed that the school should be concerned with the 'development of their personality' (70% in Disraeli), 90 against 80 per cent agreed in relation to 'gaining examination success', 84 against 74 per cent agreed on teaching 'right and wrong', 61 against 53 per cent on 'avoiding trouble in class', 87 against 74 per cent on 'getting on with others', and 100 against 95 per cent on 'getting a good job'. Bevan's pupils had increased their pro-school views more than Disraeli students, especially in respect to their increased confidence in the staff, and were more optimistic about prospects after leaving school, with 63 to 44 per cent respectively of students having the aspiration to 'go to college or university', an encouraging finding for both schools, reflecting the quality and commitment of the comparative school.

Searching for 'value added': Disadvantaged children as teenagers

The above general results are encouraging, but how well did the core, socio-economically disadvantaged children in the project do? To test this, data were extrapolated on the Attlee 14–16-year-olds, to compare with pupils from another run-down estate, Beta Park, who were now at Disraeli (see Table 4.3). Bevan had 13 per cent (48) ex-Attlee 14–16-year-olds, and Disraeli had 36 per cent (180) ex-Beta-Park students. Apart from the ex-Attlee pupils having more unemployed fathers (56% to 38%), the two samples were a reasonably close social match.

The ex-Attlee adolescents had significantly less problematic behaviour than the ex-Beta-Park teenagers did on all measures except smoking, for which levels were high in both groups.

Table 4.3 Comparison of core disadvantaged children

Problems	Ex-Attlee n=48 (%)	Ex-Beta-Park n=180 (%)
Truants often	15	39 ***
Fights often	15	29 ***
Vandalism	13	22 *
All theft	22	53 ***
Solvents	2	10 **
Cannabis	21	25
Hard drugs	0	12 ***
Hard drugs often	0	7 *
Liked school	77	57 ***
Wish for college/ University	52	33 **

These results strongly suggest that the project school integrated those inherently disadvantaged young people better than the comparative school. The most heartening finding was the improvement in hard-drug misuse, as previously the Attlee estate was notorious for drug dealing and its high rate of drug seizures. Moreover, the ex-Attlee group was significantly more positive about school, 77 against 57 per cent reporting that they liked school. Thus, from a comparison of their behaviour and attitudes, the project teenagers from the most disadvantaged backgrounds reported important value-added features in their behaviour and attitudes.

Educational outcomes

The schools under review were not 'mixed ability', being near single-sex grammar schools, a fact to be borne in mind in assessing their GCSE results. The proportion of Bevan's pupils achieving at least C grade in five GCSEs rose from 20 to 37 per cent over the period, their best-ever result. Disraeli went from 13 to 20 per cent, also one of their best-ever years, but a national newspaper identified Bevan as one of the ten most improved state schools in England. This 'external' assessment of the improvements in Bevan school was further confirmed by an independent but confidential Health Authority study on drug misuse in the county in the last year of the project. This reported very similar social characteristics and drug misuse rates to those found by us, with respect to the secondary schools under review. Moreover, it showed that in relative terms both our schools, especially Bevan, had moved to a lower than county average for drug misuse.

Parental interest in their children's education increased over the period of the project. In the third year all parents in the project schools attended a school function for a non-disciplinary reason at least once. This 'enthused' and energised the teachers, and was a clear demonstration of the improvement of family–school collaboration. It was also clear that disliking school was associated in important ways with problematic behaviour. In the surveys the emphasis had been upon problematic behaviour. The data were re-analysed to identify which groups had the *lowest* level of delinquent behaviour. The data were regrouped as follows: all secondary students who said they 'liked school', compared to the rest; children from two-parent families, compared to those from single parent families; and students with an employed father, compared to the rest. While problematic behaviour was proportionally lower in the two-parent than the one-parent families, and in families where the father was employed, the *lowest* level of delinquent behaviour came from the students who said they enjoyed school, even though this group contained 29 per cent single-parent-family students and 27 per cent with unemployed fathers. This was an unequivocal indicator of the developmental importance of enhancing students' attachment to school.

It must be reiterated that no one single finding of the evaluation stands alone. However, there is clear indicative evidence that the school-based family service schools performed better than the comparative schools over the period. Bearing in mind the social context in which the schools operated, these improvements are very encouraging. The final question is, however: Can this level of service, which costs £59,000 p.a., be afforded?

Cost–benefit analysis

Education budget savings are based upon comparing numbers of children excluded from school with those transferred into the four schools, and then looking at the cost of special educational provision – either home tuition or an admission to an educational behavioural disturbed unit (EBDU). Table 4.4 shows the numbers of children excluded, and transferred-in children, from the four schools over the period.

Table 4.4 Savings from project, comparative exclusions and new entrants				
Schools	Entered	Excluded	Gains +/–	Likely savings
Attlee savings +	28	0	+28	+£230,300
Churchill costs -	3	10	–7	–£51,700
Bevan savings +	37	9	+28	+£217,700
Disraeli savings +	14	8	+6	+£49,200

Project v. control schools' exclusions and transfers by each year: $\chi^2 = 13.2057$, 5 d/f. Yates correction applied, $P = <0.05$. All exclusions and transfers, project v. control: $\chi^2 = 19.66$, 1 d/f, $P = <0.0001$.

The project schools, significantly, excluded fewer and took 78 per cent of all problematic transfers over the period. Attlee had a net gain of 28, which in terms of likely costs saved is estimated at £230,300 over the three years, whereas Churchill had a net 'loss' of problem children, with further costs of approximately £51,700 to the education budget. Disraeli's undoubted 'community' orientation was seen in its overall saving, estimated at £49,200. However, Bevan's 28 net gains yielded four times this estimate, £217,700.

In year 3, the Ofsted inspector independently reported that 25 of the Attlee primary children required some special education. If Attlee had excluded these children the local provision would have been overwhelmed. In year 3 alone, taking a cautious position in estimating the savings on pupils going to an EBDU and staying for an average six months, the minimal estimated Attlee saving would be £56,700, and Bevan's £30,500, an overall saving of £87,200.

The reduction in delinquency can also be calculated in terms of cost savings. Ignoring the lower drug, vandalism and truancy rates of Bevan, we concentrate here only upon the Bevan students involved in theft. If they had stolen at the rate of Disraeli students, in addition to the 95 Bevan students who reported stealing, there would have been a further 168 offenders. Using Coopers and Lybrand's rates only as an indication of potential saving, the estimated figure for savings to the criminal justice system is in excess of £400,000, and this is based on the average of the costs of attending court, and does not include the cost to the victim (Coopers and Lybrand 1994).

However, assuming that most adolescent theft does not cost the same as 'adult' crime, we compared only those most at risk of a criminal career, i.e. those from disadvantaged backgrounds who had attended Attlee and Beta Park. In the event, their theft rates were 22 and 53 per cent respectively. The differential in terms of numbers of offenders suggests a 'saving' of 14 offenders, which, on the Coopers and Lybrand basis, yields a notional saving of £37,800. However, a coterminous but separate study of 16–17-year offenders in the county, who are only a year on from our 14–16-year-olds, found 183 older adolescent offenders, the cost of whose offending was estimated as £854,000, an average of £4600 each for the year (Pritchard and Cox 1997), close to the Audit Commission's (1996) estimates. Moreover, there is evidence to show that 50 per cent of inmates of Young Offenders Institutions have at some time been excluded from school (HM Chief Inspector of Prisons 1997; Lyon *et al.* 2000), reinforcing the point that our estimates of cost are cautious and conservative. Consequently the claimed £37,800 'delinquency' savings for the ex-Attlee pupils is a very modest estimate indeed. Continuing on the side of caution, and including only the minimal savings to criminal justice of £37,800, and the £87,200 education 'savings', after deducting the annual cost of the project, we are looking at an estimated gross saving in excess of £65,700, or a 111 per cent return on the 'investment'.

This does not seem an excessive claim, especially when remembering the potential intergenerational implications, and the savings to social services and health budgets, which are excluded from the estimate. Exclusion, however, carries not only a cost to education, but also to the criminal justice system. In a separate study which analysed police records of a five-year cohort of former excluded-from-school adolescents, now aged 16–23 (N = 227), it was found that 63 per cent had criminal convictions. This cost the criminal justice system a minimum of £4.2 million, or £30,000 per pupil (Pritchard and Cox 1998). Consequently, if we projected forward the reduced delinquency and exclusions from the project schools, instead of the 111 per cent return on the preventive investment, the return might – still cautiously – be claimed to be more than 250 per cent. In minimal cash terms, this is in excess of half a million pounds per two-year cohort.

The cost of failure

The Chief Officers were so impressed with the results, they incorporated the project into the secondary school, but they raised the question: What does it cost when we fail to intervene and divert potential delinquents from progressing onto the usual cycle of crime, early pregnancy, substance misuse, etc.? To set the success of the project in context, therefore, we measured the 'cost of failure', defined as an adolescent being permanently excluded from school. We saw above that a cohort of young people excluded from school had, by the age of 23, already cost £4.2 million; and of course their criminal careers were not complete – a third had already been to prison and a third were currently being processed in the criminal justice system. However, 10 per cent of the cohort were or had been in local authority care, and we assumed that their outcomes would be worse than for the group as a whole (Biehal *et al.* 1995). On investigation, however, it turned out that the ex-care group had better outcomes. This surprising finding led to a direct comparison of a five-year cohort of ex-care adolescents (n = 814) with the excluded-from-school cohort both in terms of their 'criminality' and their subsequent victimisation by crime or suicide.

Of the formerly excluded cohort 63 per cent had a criminal record, compared with 36 per cent of the ex-care group. Amongst the males, 58 per cent of the excluded group had convictions for violence, compared with 48 per cent of the ex-care group, while the 'core' offenders, responsible for 80 per cent of each group's offences, made up 23 per cent of the excluded group and 18 per cent of the ex-care group. Moreover, while 49 per cent of the excluded group had not been convicted within the last two years, 73 per cent of the ex-care group were conviction-free. If the excluded group had offended at the rate of the ex-care group, the cost to the system would have been £2.7 million, not £4.2 million.

Nonetheless, within this cost of failure are important indicators of areas of success. The ex-care young people had the benefit of statutory supervision and support, whereas the excluded group got – and continue to get – nothing. This counts as further evidence that (good) social work works. The vitally important research of Biehal *et al.* (1995) led to the call by Sir William Utting (1999) to do something for young people who had already 'lost their childhood', but this research was unnecessarily gloomy because the authors did not compare young people leaving care with another group of disadvantaged youngsters. This is not to say that young people leaving care do not have considerable disadvantages. For example, our cohort, as well as committing more crime than the general population, had a significantly higher rate of crime committed against them, as did the excluded-from-school group, among whom young women were far more likely to be victims of violent and sexual crime. The ex-care group included a number of victims of homicide, and had a rate of homicide victimisation far in excess of the general population rate (33 times as high for males and an incredible 73 times as high for females). Conversely, an area where the ex-care group might have been expected to score worse was in relation to suicide, because being in care is associated with suicidal behaviour (Pritchard 1999). Over the five years, there were no suicides in this group, whereas the males excluded from school had a subsequent suicide rate 15 times that of the general population (Pritchard and Butler 2000b).

What can be said with confidence, then, is that if we fail to integrate young people into society, which means we have to 'compensate' them for the invariable cycle of parental failures, then not only do they add to the ranks of the socially excluded – they cost society dear.

Conclusions

Nevertheless, good social work, adequately resourced and supported, can bring about change, as shown in the range of evidence presented that a school-based service can reinforce and/or compensate for parental care, improve attachment to education and, therefore, employment prospects, and serve as a barrier against a delinquent career. The project's effort to maintain problematic children within mainstream education coincided with the majority of parental aspirations and provided an important plank in the child/parent/worker relationship, as demonstrated in the consumer responses. This strengthened those protective factors in positive family, peer and school relationships. In essence the child and family social work project was a catalyst, enhancing parental supervision and the professionalism of teacher colleagues. It actively sought to strengthen parental aspirations for their children, reaffirming their worth as people and parents, empowering them to have the optimism to provide a more socially coherent and less coercive home, and helping them to break into the vicious cycle.

A key factor in the project was the speedy availability of the social worker to child, family and school. This early intervention meant avoiding the build-up of intra-classroom tensions, so disruptive to others, and thus facilitated the work of teachers and school, enhancing all pupils' education. The orientation of the project made a major contribution to the ethos of the school by showing that, having first dealt with the emergencies, it was possible to move towards an integrated psycho-socio-educational preventive approach to reduce crises. This further developed the community orientation of the schools, enhancing many aspects of school life, which in turn demonstrated the importance of the school to the wider community.

It is conceded that the project team was operating in an optimal professional situation – with a reasonable level of resources and good support, but with minimal bureaucracy. This released their creative professional capacities, so they worked flexibly and at times more convenient for families than the usual office hours. The project released, activated and encouraged the professional potential within the schools. This reduced the alienation of potentially vulnerable children, which created a virtuous cycle of dialogue between parents, school and agencies.

The key target and primary 'beneficiaries' of the project were the children, as seen in their improved behaviour and educational achievements, and in parents who took a more active part in school life and valued the proactive stance of the school. There are six main interactive findings emerging from the project.

1. The project was strategically placed to meet the needs of troubled and vulnerable children and families in a non-stigmatising way. This was seen in improvements of the children's behaviour, family functioning, and the development of inter-agency collaboration.

2. The accessible and acceptable school-based crisis team contributed to the school's role as a socialising agency. Their availability to teachers contributed to their morale and their education of the children.

3. The team's situation was close to the professional optimum: they were supported, with minimal bureaucracy and an adequate resource base. This energised them, enhancing their ability to respond to child and family.

4. That 'liking school' was a barrier against teenage delinquency confirmed the value-added aspect of the compensatory potential of schools. This was despite the fact that a significant minority of the children belonged to disadvantaged families.

5. Despite the weaknesses in the cost–benefit analysis, there can be little doubt that the project contributed to a reduction of exclusions, improved identification with school, and produced measurable financial savings. Thus this preventive investment project met most of its objectives of trying to reverse the vicious cycle, as the family/teacher/social-work alliance contributed to the reduction of truancy and delinquency, enhancing the children's life opportunities to be better citizens and future parents.

6. From the qualitative evaluation, the teachers' and pupils' questionnaires and interviews, the importance of trust and confidence in the relationship became clear. This was amply demonstrated in a separate consumer study of truants and their parents, and the 90 per cent participation rate spoke volumes for

the way in which they valued their social worker. This was summed up beautifully by a 14-year-old, who wrote: 'I enjoyed doing this kestonair, it helped me to see how much better I am and it showed me that blokes can be just a good as women at listening.'

With such positive results it is perhaps not surprising that the previous government acknowledged that the project is one of the most 'promising innovations' which can contribute to a reduction in crime (Home Office 1997a). Indeed, the present government incorporated the project into its White Paper *Reducing Youth Crime in England* (Home Office 1997b). Perhaps such projects might receive the resources and professional support necessary in view of what has long been known about education helping to reduce crime (Rose and Marshall 1974; Rutter *et al.* 1979; Farrington 1995; Rutter and Smith 1995; Audit Commission 1998); the evidence of the effectiveness of a school-based child and family social work service; and the political aspiration to be 'tough on the causes of crime'. All that is lacking is the political will to maximise the cost–benefit results, which would save society money and future victims their distress, and empower young people to fuller citizenship and personal development, so that we can join with Wordsworth in the fifth book of *The Prelude*, and speak of 'A race of real children, not too wise,/Too learned, or too good; but wanton, fresh,/ And bandied up and down by love and hate…May books and nature be their early joy,/And knowledge, rightly honoured with that name,/Knowledge not purchased by the loss of power'.

References

Akehurst, M., Brown, I. and Wessley, S. (1995) *Dying for Help: Offenders at Risk of Suicide.* Wakefield: Association of Chief Probation Officers.

Audit Commission (1996) *Misspent Youth – Young People and Crime.* London: Audit Commission.

Audit Commission (1998) *Misspent Youth 1998: The Challenge for Youth Justice.* London: Audit Commission.

Biehal, N., Clayden, J. and Stein, M. (1995) *Moving On: Young People Leaving Care.* London: HMSO.

Blyth, E. and Milner, J. (1998) *Social Work with Children.* London: Heinemann.

Boateng, P. (2000) 'Foreword' to *The National Strategy for Neighbourhood Renewal, Report 12: Young People.* London: The Stationery Office.

Borg, M.G., Riding, R.J. and Falzon, J.M. (1991) 'Stress in teaching: A study of occupational stress and its determinants, job satisfaction and career commitments among primary school teachers.' *International Journal of Educational Psychology 11*, 59–75.

Coopers and Lybrand (1994) *Preventative Strategy for Young People in Trouble.* London: Prince's Trust.

Department of Employment (1992–97) *Employment Gazette April/July.* London: HMSO.

Department of Health (1998) *A Healthier Nation.* London: HMSO.

Dupper, D.R. (1998) 'An alternative to suspension for middle-school youths with behavioural problems: Findings from a School Survival group.' *Research on Social Work Practice 8*, 3, 354–366.

Farrington, D.P. (1995) 'The development of offending and anti-social behaviour from childhood: Key findings from the Cambridge Study in Delinquent Development.' *Journal of Child Psychology and Psychiatry 36*, 929–964.

Goldblatt, P. and Lewis, C. (1998) *Reducing Offending: An Assessment of Research Evidence on Ways of Dealing with Offending Behaviour* (Home Office Research Study 187). London: Home Office.

Graham, J. and Bowling, B. (1995) *Young People and Crime.* London: Home Office.

HM Chief Inspector of Prisons (1997) *Young Prisoners: A Thematic Review.* London: HMIP.

Home Office (1997a) *Reducing Youth Crime: A Consultative Document.* London: Home Office.

Home Office (1997b) *No More Excuses: New Approaches to Young Crime in England.* London: Home Office.

Home Office (1998) *The Prison Population in 1997: A Statistical Review* (Research Findings 76). London: Home Office.

Lyon, J., Dennison, C. and Wilson, A. (2000) *'Tell Them So They Listen': Messages from Young People in Custody* (Home Office Research Study 201). London: Home Office.

Mindle, J.S. (1995) 'Tobacco advertising.' *Journal of the Royal Society of Health 115*, 84–89.

Morgan, C. and Murgatroyd, S. (1994) *Total Quality Management Perspective in the Public Sector.* Buckingham: Open University Press.

OFSTED (1993) *Education for Disaffected Pupils.* London: Department of Education.

O'Keefe, D. (1994) *Truancy in English Secondary Schools.* London: HMSO.

Patterson, G.R. (1994) 'Alternative to seven myths about treating families of antisocial Children.' In C. Henricson (ed.) *Crime and the Family.* London: Family Policy Studies Centre, 26–49.

Policy Action Team (2000) *The National Strategy for Neighbourhood Renewal: Report 12: Young People.* London: The Stationery Office.

Pritchard, C. (1999) *Suicide: The Ultimate Rejection? A Psychosocial Study.* Buckingham: Open University Press.

Pritchard, C. (2001) *A Family-Teacher-Social Worker Alliance to Reduce Truancy and Delinquency: The Dorset Healthy Alliance Project* (RDS Occasional Paper 78). London: Home Office.

Pritchard, C. and Butler, A. (2000a) 'A follow-up study of crime, murder and the cost of crime in English cohorts of former excluded-from-school and in-care adolescents.' *International Journal of Adolescent Medicine and Health 12*, 223–244.

Pritchard, C. and Butler, A. (2000b) 'A follow-up study of victims of crime, murder and suicide in cohorts of English former excluded-from-school and in-care adolescents.' *International Journal of Adolescent Medicine and Health 12*, 275–294.

Pritchard, C. and Cox, M. (1997) *Evaluating a Bail Support Scheme for Young Adults.* Dorchester: Dorset Probation Service.

Pritchard, C. and Cox, M. (1998) 'Subsequent criminality of former excluded-from-school adolescents as young adults 16–23: Costs and missed opportunities.' *Journal of Adolescence 21*, 5, 609–620.

Pritchard, C., Cotton, A. and Cox, M. (1992a) 'Truancy, drug abuse and knowledge of HIV infection in 926 normal adolescents.' *Journal of Adolescence 15*, 1, 1–17.

Pritchard, C., Cotton, A., Godson, D., Cox, M. and Weeks, S. (1992b) 'Mental illness, drug and alcohol misuse and HIV risk behaviour in 214 young adult probation clients.' *Social Work and Social Sciences Review 3*, 2, 150–162.

Pritchard, C., Dawson, A. and Cox, M. (1997) 'Suicide and violent death in a six year cohort of male probationers compared with general male population mortality: Evidence of accumulative socio-psychiatric vulnerability.' *Journal of the Royal Society of Health 117*, 180–185.

Pritchard, C. and Taylor, R. (1978) *Social Work: Reform or Revolution?* London: Routledge and Kegan Paul.

Pritchard, C., Williams, R., Cotton, A. and Bowen, D. (1998) 'A consumer study of adolescents' views of their education social worker: Engagement v. non-engagement as an indicator of effective relationships.' *British Journal of Social Work 28*, 6, 915–938.

Pritchard, C. and Williams, R. (2001) 'A three-year comparative longitudinal study of a school-based social work family service to reduce truancy, delinquency and school exclusions.' *Journal of Social Welfare and Family Law 23*, 1, 23–43.

Pyle, D.J. and Deadman, D.F. (1994) 'Crime and the business cycle in post-war Britain.' *British Journal of Criminology 34*, 3, 339–352.

Rose, G. and Marshall, T.F. (1974) *Counselling and School Social Work.* London: Wiley.

Rutter, M., Maughan, S. and Smith, A. (1979) *15,000 Hours: Secondary Schools and their Impact upon Children.* London: Open Books.

Rutter, M. and Smith, D.J. (eds) (1995) *Psychosocial Disorders in Young People: Time Trends and their Causes.* Chichester: Wiley.

Rutter, M., Giller, H. and Hagell, A. (1998) *Antisocial Behaviour in Young People.* Cambridge: Cambridge University Press.

Social Exclusion Unit (1998) *Truancy and School Exclusion.* London: HMSO.

Utting, D. (1999) *Communities that Care: Evidence of Good Practice to Reduce Crime.* London: Social Exclusion Unit.

CHAPTER 5

Domestic Violence

Evidence-Led Policy – Ignorance-Led Practice?

Julie Taylor-Browne

Introduction

In the past ten years there have been a significant number of investigations and evaluations of what reduces domestic violence. The findings are discussed in this chapter and show that effective interventions by housing authorities, police and health personnel can persuade women that they can be protected, resettled where necessary and supported by appropriate agencies. It is surprising, therefore, that awareness and implementation of these strategies are not more widespread. Given what is known about both the effects and the huge costs of domestic violence, this lack of evidence-based practice raises the question of why statutory agencies seem so reluctant to take on the task of tackling domestic violence. The benefits to the agencies themselves and to the people involved are obvious both in terms of human suffering and of financial cost.

Too often, it seems, professionals feel overwhelmed by women's apparent inability or reluctance to 'sort themselves out' and to break free from their abusers. Statutory workers feel themselves unable to meet the many and varied needs of women victims, which may include re-housing, child care, transport, legal advice and, not infrequently, protection for the family pet. In the time allotted for a consultation with a general medical practitioner, or during an emergency call for the police, professionals trying to help victims of domestic violence may well feel that they are failing to offer adequate support. This feeling may be compounded by subsequent, and sometimes numerous, encounters with the same women, manifesting similar or escalating needs.

Nevertheless, there is research illustrating that appropriate responses, advice and referrals can significantly reduce the amount of violence a woman may suffer. Knowing the right strategies to put into place can also liberate individual agency workers from feeling overwhelmed with the task of helping a woman, and instead offers them appropriate and targeted responses to a domestic violence 'case'. This chapter reviews work carried out on women victims, children affected by domestic violence, and male perpetrators. Because the vast majority of serious domestic violence incidents are committed by men against women (Mirrlees-Black 1999), there has been little robust research carried out on male victims, female perpetrators or violence within same-sex relationships. This is not to say, however, such violence does not exist. Similarly, there is also a dearth of research (particularly quantitative work) on violence against disabled women or those in ethnic minority communities (see, however, Mama (1996) and Rai and Thiara (1997) on the needs of black women, and Young *et al.* (1997) on the prevalence of abuse among disabled women).

This chapter will demonstrate that there is a substantial quantity of research evidence from the UK, the USA and elsewhere that shows the way forward in tackling domestic violence. Much of this material has been published and publicised by central government,[1] yet there seems to be little evidence to indicate that these recommendations have been noticed, let alone implemented (see Hanmer *et al.* 1999; Plotnikoff and Woolfson 1998; Grace 1995; Morley and Mullender 1994; Smith 1989; Home Office 1990, 1995, 2000).

What is known about domestic violence?

First, it is widespread, affecting (although not in equal measure) women of all ages, income brackets and ethnic origins. Nearly a quarter of women have experienced domestic violence in their lifetime (Mirrlees-Black 1999). These are rarely single incidents and the course of domestic violence may run for a number of years before help is sought from statutory agencies. Violence frequently escalates over time, with subsequent effects on health, employment and children.

Risk factors for abuse

In a review of relevant literature Walby and Myhill (2001) found that increased risk for domestic violence was associated with the following factors:

- *Previous assault.* A number of studies on repeat victimisation, for example on burglary and car crime, have found that one incident of victimisation is an excellent predictor of subsequent incidents. These studies also found that the next victimisation would follow shortly after the first (e.g. Farrell and Pease 1993). The same pattern appears to hold for domestic violence victimisation. Lloyd *et al.* (1994), for example, found that 62 per cent of all police calls to domestic incidents were from households from which there had been one or more previous such calls in a two-year period; and that 35 per cent of households suffered a second incident within five weeks of the first.

- *Separation.* A number of studies indicate that women who are separated from the partners or husbands have a significantly higher risk of domestic violence than those in other marital statuses. Staff in agencies dealing with child custody or child visitation arrangements, child support arrangements, and housing need to be aware of this, factoring in the protective strategies needed for this stage.

- *Socio-economic status/ill health and disability.* While domestic violence undoubtedly occurs in families who are better off, it is linked to lower household income, unemployment, those families experiencing financial difficulties and those where the women's income in particular is low. Women suffering from ill health and disabilities are also at greater risk from victimisation.

- *Gender inequality and patriarchal attitudes.* A number of studies have shown that where a woman is dependent on her partner (for example where she has young children, earns a small proportion of the family's income or does not work at all), her risk of victimisation is increased. There is also a correlation between an acceptance of a man's right to use violence against women and the use of actual violence. Thus a common feature of perpetrator programmes is a challenging of these attitudes.

- *Age of the victim and perpetrator.* Studies show that the risk of being a victim of or a perpetrator of domestic violence decreases with age. Because younger women are disproportionately affected, violence is likely to occur during pregnancy and the period of child rearing, which clearly has implications for the health and social services.

- *Child abuse.* There is overwhelming evidence to support the co-occurrence of domestic violence and child abuse. This incorporates all forms of abuse, with the perpetrator of one being the perpetrator of the other.

- *Violence in family of origin.* Many studies have found that there is a correlation between growing up in a family that suffers domestic violence and going on to become a perpetrator in later life. However, this appears not to be of sufficient predictive value for preventive action to be taken unless it is combined with other factors such as an anti-social personality and patriarchal values.

In a similar review of factors identified in the USA, Low *et al.* (2002) confirm these risk factors and identify the additional ones of cohabitation before marriage, race, alcohol use (or overuse) and lack of social support/networks.

Evaluated interventions

A number of interventions have been evaluated in the UK and elsewhere, and in addition the results of the Home Office crime reduction programme Violence Against Women Initiative, due shortly, should further increase our knowledge.[2] It is appropriate that the search for best and most effective practice should continue to be funded, since domestic violence incidents account for a quarter of all reported/recorded crime in the UK (Mirrlees-Black *et al.* 1996), and the crimes committed and their consequences consume vast resources (Stanko *et al.* 1998).

What research there has been into how to help women effectively can be broken down into the areas of service delivery. An alternative way to look at these interventions would be to analyse the points of potential intervention along the primary, secondary and tertiary frameworks. This would allow strategies to be developed along the lines of: working to prevent the abuse from happening at all (primary prevention or intervention); intervening quickly to prevent immediate harm and to prevent a recurrence (secondary interventions); and helping those who have suffered harm to ameliorate its effects (tertiary interventions). This last approach would be highly relevant to those designing a multi-agency strategy, but for the purposes of describing evaluated initiatives, the focus has been on the first two approaches.

Work with children

Large numbers of children whose mothers suffer domestic violence are at risk, a fact well known to social services. There is a startlingly large overlap between the presence of domestic violence in the home and the children's suffering some form of abuse – covering neglect and physical, sexual and emotional abuse (Mullender 2001). This points to a clear need for practitioners in both child protection and domestic violence spheres to work closely together to prevent these crimes, to identify them earlier and to work with the non-abusing parent and the children to ensure their safety.

There is some evidence on preventing harm to children and ameliorating harm that has already occurred, although little of this research has tracked the effects of interventions over a follow-up period. Clearly there are practical and ethical difficulties in conducting research that isolates a single variable (such as counselling) and studies its effect. Added to this are the difficulties inherent in specifying both a follow-up period and what the appropriate outcome measures should be. There are, however, some evidence-based clues as to early identification, protection and prevention. Additionally, there is also some evidence as to the consequences of domestic violence. Many studies show that those who have experienced it suffer from increased anxiety, depression, aggression and conflict disorder; children may also blame themselves and feel responsible for the violence. Later consequences include an increased risk of dating violence: that is, boys from an abusive background were more likely to commit it, and girls from an abusive background to be victims of it (McGee *et al.* 1997; for a comprehensive review of evaluations of interventions see Graham-Bermann (2001)). Encouragingly, a number of these evaluations show that work with children can change their attitudes to violence, decrease anxiety, reduce conflict with peers, and increase self-esteem.

The interventions offered vary as to the setting (for example, they may take place at home or in a shelter), and as to the subject of the intervention (for example, this may be the abused child alone, the child and siblings, or the child and mother). Commonly the programmes offered cover issues of blame, fear and secrecy, and explore protective strategies and alternative ways of dealing with conflict. Interventions are age-appropriate; so, for example, programmes for pre-school-age children may use story-telling techniques and puppets. More participatory methods are used for older children, such as creating and acting in a play. Work with teenagers may focus on devising messages for the community or on appropriate dating behaviour.

In relation to preventive work, research has been carried out on attitudes to domestic violence among children and young people. A survey of 2039 young people aged 14–21 found that nearly a half of the young men and a third of the young women surveyed thought there could be circumstances in which it would be acceptable for a man to hit his female partner (Burton and Kitzinger 1998). Partly as a consequence of studies such as this, there are now a number of packages (including drama presentations) developed for use in schools' physical health and social education classes aimed at preventing domestic violence. Mullender (1994) notes, however, that these approaches are more effective when delivered not in isolation but through a 'whole community' approach involving not only parents, school staff and relevant services but also other community groups and media campaigns. Prevention campaigns evaluated in the USA and reviewed by Avery-Leaf and Cascardi (2002) indicate that school-based partner-violence prevention programmes are effective in affecting help-seeking behaviours, conflict behaviours and self-ratings of relationship skills. Their recommendations as to implementing prevention programmes are summarised as follows (p.100):

- target whole populations
- train existing personnel to administer programmes
- maintain a gender-neutral focus, especially in mixed-gender classrooms
- begin skills training early
- target attitude change
- provide booster sessions after programme is complete
- include peer counselling.

Prevention work with couples

Studies in the USA reviewed by Low *et al.* (2002) indicate that pre-marriage courses which include modules on violence in marriage and conflict resolution have been shown to be effective in reducing the number of aggressive incidents compared with that found in control samples. Further, early intervention with couples who wish to work together on the issue by attendance on a more targeted course have also resulted in a reduction in further violent incidents.

Perpetrators

Work with perpetrators, where this exists, is largely carried out by the probation service, although there are a number of programmes provided by the voluntary sector. There has been some debate over the years about the content of the programmes, although it is now generally accepted that programmes should be based around cognitive change. Couples work, drug and alcohol dependency, and anger management should not be addressed within these programmes, although there may often be a requirement for such additional needs to be addressed in addition to the domestic violence issues. There is also a need for parallel programmes (or at least services) to support the partners of those attending programmes. Obtaining the truth regarding re-abuse, aligning expectations with reality and ensuring safety are but three of the key needs of women whose partners are undertaking a cognitive change programme (Burton *et al.* 1998; Dobash *et al.* 2000).

RESPECT (2000) makes a number of good practice recommendations, including the minimum length of a programme (which should be at least 75 hours over 30 weeks), who should facilitate the course, and the training the facilitators should receive.

However, programmes for perpetrators are few and far between, and there is a heated debate about whether resources for programmes could be better spent on interventions focused on the women victims. This debate is fuelled by the equivocal findings on 'success' rates. Mullender and Burton (2001) discuss this fully, but the difficulties of getting men into programmes and then sustaining their attendance mean that the numbers who complete programmes and can be followed up for a meaningful length of time are small, making it difficult to claim any statistical significance for the results. (The Australian National Campaign against Violence and Crime Unit (1998) recommends a follow-up period of at least twelve months.) So, is it possible to say anything about whether perpetrator programmes work or not? The most that can be said is that results are moderately encouraging – for those who complete the course, with a 'modest effect in reducing repeat offending' (see the review by Healey and Smith (1998)). The methods used to measure success are important, of course, and the use of partner reports is essential.

A key issue for those considering setting up perpetrator programmes is how to address the very high non-completion rates of men on perpetrator programmes and how to deal with those who reoffend whilst on the programme. Evidence shows that re-abuse tends to happen very early on in the course of the programme. Another issue is that of voluntary attenders on programmes – should they attend the same programmes as court-mandated offenders? What is the effect on outcomes for either group when they are mixed and worked with separately? There is still much that is not known about perpetrator programmes, and until we find ways to motivate abusers to continue through to the completion of a programme – either through a 'stick approach' such as the issue of an arrest warrant (Gondolf 1998) or through a 'carrot' approach such as one-to-one support by an established attender (Burton *et al.* 1998) – the effectiveness of programmes in reducing victimisation will remain unproven.

Health

The scope for the health sector to be a key agency in successful interventions in domestic violence is huge, and there are some indications that an appreciation of this is beginning to permeate a sector that traditionally has been slow to respond to change. The Department of Health and the professional bodies for health professionals have all issued guidance on this issue (e.g. Department of Health 2000). The health costs of domestic violence are enormous and are incurred through general practitioners' surgeries, emergency medical services, mental health provision, substance abuse, antenatal care, plastic surgery, dental services, and gynaecological and neonatal settings.

Health professionals also see women, children and families routinely (e.g. for ante- and postnatal care and vaccinations) and regularly (for contraceptive advice and childhood illnesses and accidents). In rural areas, where women may have access to no other services, the health sector is of particular importance (Mullins *et al.* 2000; Short *et al.* 2002), but what are busy midwives, doctors, dentists and accident-and-emergency unit nurses to do when confronted (sometimes repeatedly) with a suspected victim of domestic violence?

Literature reviewed by the British Medical Association (1998) found that women want to be asked by professionals if they are being abused. They do not want to have to raise it themselves. This is in contrast to the 'screening' approach where professionals either implicitly or explicitly look for the existence of indicators of abuse, and assess whether the person in front of them is likely to be a victim. Once the victim has been identified, or preferably identifies herself, pre-agreed referrals can be made, and support and information given. Whatever method is used, women will only risk disclosing that they are victims of abuse to an appropriately trained and sympathetic staff member – in the absence of the perpetrator – and they must be able to feel reassured about confidentiality.

Nonetheless, there is evidence that health professionals find it difficult to ask women about domestic violence and do not feel equipped to deal with a positive response. There is an identified need for training, awareness-raising and appropriate resourcing. Short *et al.* (2002) describe a programme in the USA where independent support personnel were provided within hospitals. In a two-year period, 1719 domestic violence victims were referred to the support service (WomenKind), compared with 27 victims who were referred to trained social workers in hospitals without a specific support service. The team worked on the basis that health professionals fail to intervene because:

- they have little or no training to help them recognise the signs of domestic abuse

- they are uncomfortable intervening with a victim of abuse

- they do not see such interventions as their responsibility

- they do not have the time or the resources needed to assist the victim of abuse.

Other interventions have relied on hospital staff to refer to agencies based outside the hospital and who do not routinely work with them. These have had mixed success. Davidson *et al.* (2001) conducted a review of these and found that health care professionals had a higher rate of identifying victims when they used a routine screening tool, that is, a series of questions which asked directly about whether the woman had suffered domestic violence, abuse in pregnancy, or forced sexual activity. Other studies examined the impact of training and awareness-raising among staff and found that, unless these activities are ongoing, the use of the screening tool and referrals will diminish over time.

The health sector is unique in having regular access to families where both prevention and early identification can take place. Health settings can not only be used to advertise independent support services; they can also offer proactive help using regular, routine screening and referrals, and offer confidential, non-judgemental support. Clearly there are issues to be resolved about ensuring that there are services to which women can be referred; and there is also a further shift to be made in encouraging health staff to believe that it is part of their role, and providing them with appropriate (and repeated) awareness-raising, training and support. As the health service becomes more and more aware of the enormous cost of picking up the pieces of women's lives, it is inevitable that it will move into this sphere.

Policing domestic violence

The police are one of the most important agencies in responding to and preventing further domestic violence. Often they are one of the first agencies turned to, and their role is key. In the USA there has been much discussion about the use of 'mandatory arrest' policies whereby the police arrest perpetrators when answering a call to a domestic violence incident. Because of criticism of this approach (e.g. Zorza 1995), many police forces in the UK and elsewhere have adopted a 'positive arrest' policy, whereby the presumption is that an arrest will be made, although the police have some discretion. While this debate will run and run, it is clear that women need protection at that time, in the immediate aftermath of a violent incident; they may wish to initiate prosecution, but it is more than likely that they need access to information and support services. It is essential that both perpetrator and victim know that efforts are being made by agencies to end the violence.

Some forces in the UK – for example, West Yorkshire – have experimented with letters to the perpetrator and advice to women on where to go for further help (Hanmer *et al.* 1999). Successful evaluations of alarms and mobile phones issued to women are reviewed by Hanmer and Griffiths (2001), but the most convincing is the approach of policing domestic violence through repeat victimisation. This approach accepts that historically, repeated calls to the same family have resulted in a poorer response with each subsequent visit, as the family becomes labelled as 'just a domestic' or a 'problem family'. The repeat victimisation approach sets in place a structured pattern of increasing the level of intervention with the number of incidents. The implementation of this approach evaluated in this country (Hanmer *et al.* 1999) found that repeat victimisation fell, and that the time between victimisations increased. An additional benefit was that closer working relations developed between agencies as information was passed between them in an effort to assist the women targeted through the scheme. The message from all the police evaluations was the need to keep appropriate records so as to be able to judge the success of any initiative and to trace the women throughout the criminal justice service or to any other referral.

Housing

Feedback from women summarised by Levison and Harwin (2001) reveals that women have definite housing needs that are not currently being met by housing bodies. They express a need for accommodation that:

- is suitable for children, including being close to their existing schools
- can meet the needs of those who have disabilities
- can provide safety from the perpetrator
- allows women to maintain employment, child-care arrangements and social care networks.

In many cases this type of accommodation may be their existing home, and women may need advice and assistance on how to 'stay put' while gaining protection from their abuser. For other women there may be a strong need to be accommodated well away from the area, for example, where there is a close-knit community comprising the perpetrator's relatives. This typically occurs in rural areas and among minority ethnic groups. Edwards (2001) reviews the increasing popularity of the civil remedies available under the Family Law Act 1996 and the Protection from Harassment Act 1997. Women have expressed the need for suitable transitional housing – for example, after having been accommodated in temporary or refuge accommodation, and for follow-up services or resettlement work.

Outreach and advocacy

Outreach and advocacy have a number of definitions. At a basic level, work under this heading can mean simply providing women with information to which they might otherwise not have access. Gadomski *et al.* (2001) noted that calls to a domestic violence hotline doubled following a seven-month, public-health-based campaign in a rural area in the USA. The authors also found that this was an effective way to reach men. Typically, however, outreach and advocacy services operate on a one-to-one basis and occur when a referral is made from one of the generic services, such as health, to a specialist domestic violence service. Women report (Kelly and Humphreys 2001) highly valuing these services, as they can be given information about a wide range of services and options available to them, and frequently the outreach worker and advocate can attend meetings and advocate on their behalf, and may attend court with them. The authors describe the results of two advocacy projects, Domestic Violence Matters (DVM) and the Domestic Violence Intervention Project (DVIP). These projects were effective in creating new access to services and information for women who had never been in contact with any statutory agencies and in reducing reported victimisation in those who had been referred by the police. Outreach services have also developed into new areas, such as children's and resettlement work – developments informed by direct work with women victims.

Outreach and advocacy services are clearly an essential part of any strategy to address domestic violence. In addition to specialising in domestic violence issues and assisting women referred to them from the statutory sector, they are able to reach women who have never disclosed abuse to a statutory agency – often at an early stage of their victimisation. Outreach workers can provide experience and an overview of all the agencies a woman may have to use to escape permanently from domestic violence. They can offer support throughout this process and provide much needed continuity of contact at a very difficult time. They are independent of any statutory service, and are not limited to, for example, women who have used the refuge service. By a careful targeting of their knowledge and skills, they can be used to target hard-to-reach groups, such as those living in rural areas, those in minority ethnic groups, and those who live in more affluent areas. Women suffering domestic violence are likely to have been threatened by their abusers as to the consequences of calling the police. The independence of an outreach or advocacy service means that women can contact them without fear of being pressured into a criminal prosecution, or having social services involved.

Discussion

The preceding sections have illustrated how much we actually know about domestic violence. We know who it is likely to happen to, we know how to prevent it happening again (to the same victim), we know a great deal about the type of services women need (and want), and we know which agencies are best placed to identify and offer support to women suffering and at risk from domestic violence.

This raises the question of why measures informed by this knowledge are not being implemented on a wider basis. It appears that information about effective practice is simply not reaching the professionals who are responsible for providing services, and, as a consequence, inappropriate and inadequate services are being provided. This is not to deny that there are piecemeal 'islands' of good practice, but these are generally voluntary sector-led initiatives which lurch from one funding crisis to another before finally petering out when their leading light or 'moral entrepreneur' (Becker 1963) backs out from exhaustion or frustration.

A number of explanations are available for what has been regarded in this chapter as 'ignorance-led practice'.

1. *Multi-agency working is too difficult, so suggested strategies are never adequately implemented.* It is undoubtedly the case that multi-agency arrangements have been strained in this area; see for example Burton *et al.* (1998). Hague (2001) identifies common pitfalls and problems as well as making recommendations as to the roles and responsibilities of these partnerships and their members. These include:

    (a) consultation with user groups

    (b) addressing power differentials within the group

    (c) agreeing terms of reference

    Further data on successful multi-agency work will be forthcoming from the evaluations of the crime reduction programme Violence Against Women Initiative.

2. *Adequate resources are not available or are not being made available by statutory agencies.* A number of government initiatives have targeted domestic violence, including the crime reduction programmes Safer Communities and the Partnership Development Fund. It is likely that the trend toward funding will continue as the emphasis is put firmly on the provision by statutory agencies of appropriate services.

3.   *The wrong model of domestic violence dominates multi-agency working.*
     Currently, the discourse around domestic violence is dominated
     by the criminal justice system. Kaufman *et al.* (2002) argue that
     child sexual abuse should be primarily treated as a public health
     concern. A similar argument could be made for domestic violence.
     Within this model all of the elements of the problem – primary,
     secondary and tertiary – would be dealt with, with a stronger
     emphasis on prevention (primary interventions).

4.   *Patriarchal attitudes suffuse the agencies involved in initiatives ensuring
     their failure at every level.* Plotnikoff and Woolfson (1998), Grace
     (1995) and Smith (1989) have all identified this problem within
     the police, for example. Careful selection of staff, awareness-
     raising and training are all key to tackling this problem. The
     stressful nature of the work needs to be acknowledged and
     appropriate resources and support needs to be made available to
     Domestic Violence Officers, who have to deal not only with
     repeated violence but also with the two women a week murdered
     by their current and former partners (Mirrlees-Black 1999).

5.   *No-one monitors data or evaluates whether the initiative is successful or
     not.* Crisp and Stanko (2001) and Adler (2002) outline
     approaches to evaluating domestic violence initiatives. This is
     rarely carried out at present in such a way as to provide
     meaningful data, rendering the judgement of the success or failure
     of a project either purely subjective (and subject to political will)
     or impossible. A key problem is the failure by nearly all agencies
     to collect adequate baseline data against which any strategy can
     be measured.

6.   *No-one asks women survivors what they want, so services remain
     inappropriate and underused.* There is a need for the routine
     evaluation of the services provided by the service users. This is
     growing more common across many sectors, but there is still a
     reluctance to ask 'victims' or 'survivors' about the services they
     receive or the strategies being delivered. Of course, there are
     important safety and ethical concerns to be faced, but consulting
     with survivors of domestic violence is essential for the
     development of both good and better practice. Consultation
     needs to be carried out using objective, representative and, where

appropriate, confidential mechanisms, and needs to be open to scrutiny by other agencies in order for it to be valued. Hague (2001) discusses this further.

7.   *It is not enough of a local priority to guarantee adequate commitment from statutory agencies.* Crisp and Stanko (2001) discuss the approach and data collection methods used by Crime and Disorder Partnerships in incorporating domestic violence into local Crime and Disorder Audits and Strategies. They describe a picture of inadequate and piecemeal attempts to obtain a picture of the extent of domestic violence in their local area. This is due largely to the lack of data collected on the subject by partner agencies. This is a chicken and egg situation. It appears that no-one collects data on the extent and costs of domestic violence and, as a consequence, it remains a low priority and subject to a lack of awareness among those who hold the purse strings. There is clearly a need for measures to tackle both of these failings, and once again the initiative is coming from central government through various initiatives such as the Supporting People Initiative.[3]

Conclusion

While it is important to keep exploring what works, surely the main challenge is to implement what is already known on a widespread and local basis. There is, however, a clear need to examine why this is not being done and to ensure that it is done. For too long it has been the voluntary sector that has been shouldering an unequal proportion of the task of meeting women's needs. A wholesale shift is now required which places the responsibility firmly back onto the statutory sector, while still utilising and respecting the knowledge and experience of the voluntary sector. There is scope for a fruitful and mutually beneficial partnership between the two sectors, provided that there is transparency of working, clearly defined roles and responsibilities, and agreed protocols for information sharing and monitoring of all agencies. In this way multi-agency partnerships can move away from just talking about domestic violence and can develop *and implement* better, and better-informed, practice.

Notes

1. For example, the Department of Health's manual (2000) and the material summarised by the Home Office at www.homeoffice.gov.uk/domesticviolence/brief.htm.

2. www.homeoffice.gov.uk/domesticviolence/crp.htm.

3. See www.spkweb.org.uk.

References

Adler, M. (2002) 'The utility of modelling in evaluation planning: The case of coordination of domestic violence services in Maryland.' *Evaluation and Program Planning 25*, 203–213.

Avery-Leaf, S. and Cascardi, M. (2002) 'Dating violence education: Prevention and early intervention strategies.' In P. Schewe (ed.) *Preventing Violence in Relationships: Interventions across the Life Span.* Washington, DC: American Psychological Association.

Becker, H. (1963) *Outsiders: Studies in the Sociology of Deviance.* New York: Free Press.

British Medical Association (BMA) (1998) *Domestic Violence: A Health Care Issue?* London: BMA.

Burton, S. and Kitzinger, J., with Kelly, L. and Regan, L. (1998) *Young People's Attitudes towards Violence, Sex and Relationships. Executive Summary* (Research Report 002). Edinburgh: The Zero Tolerance Charitable Trust.

Burton, S., Regan, L. and Kelly, L. (1998) *Supporting Women and Challenging Men: Lessons from the Domestic Violence Intervention Project.* Bristol: Policy Press.

Crisp, D. and Stanko, B. (2001) 'Monitoring costs and evaluating needs.' In J. Taylor-Browne (ed.) *What Works in Reducing Domestic Violence? A Comprehensive Guide for Professionals.* London: Whiting and Birch.

Davidson, L., King, V., Garcia, J. and Marchant, S. (2001) 'What role can the health services play?' In J. Taylor-Browne (ed.) *What Works in Reducing Domestic Violence? A Comprehensive Guide for Professionals.* London: Whiting and Birch.

Dobash, R., Dobash, R., Cavanagh, K. and Lewis, R. (2000) *Changing Violent Men.* London: Sage.

Department of Health (2000) *Domestic Violence: A Resource Manual for Health Care Professionals.* London: Department of Health.

Edwards, S. (2001) 'Domestic violence and harassment: An assessment of the civil remedies.' In J. Taylor-Browne (ed.) *What Works in Reducing Domestic Violence? A Comprehensive Guide for Professionals.* London: Whiting and Birch.

Farrell, G. and Pease, K. (1993) *Once Bitten, Twice Bitten: Repeat Victimization and its Implications for Crime Prevention* (Policy Research Group, Crime Prevention Unit Paper 46). London: Home Office.

Gadomski, A., Tripp, M., Wolff, D., Lewis, C. and Jenkins, P. (2001) 'Impact of a rural domestic violence campaign.' *Journal of Rural Health 17*, 3, 266–277.

Gondolf, E. (1998) 'Do batterer programs work? A 15-month follow-up of a multi-site evaluation.' *Domestic Violence Report 3*, 64–79 (June/July).

Grace, S. (1995) *Policing Domestic Violence in the 1990s* (Home Office Research Study 139). London: Home Office.

Graham-Bermann, S. (2001) 'Designing intervention evaluations for children exposed to domestic violence: Applications of research and theory.' In S. Graham-Bermann and J. Edleson (eds) *Domestic Violence in the Lives of Children: The Future of Research Intervention and Social Policy.* Washington, DC: American Psychological Association.

Hague, G. (2001) 'Multi-agency initiatives.' In J. Taylor-Browne (ed.) *What Works in Reducing Domestic Violence? A Comprehensive Guide for Professionals.* London: Whiting and Birch.

Hanmer, J., Griffiths, S. and Jerwood, D. (1999) *Arresting Evidence: Domestic Violence and Repeat Victimisation* (Police Research Series 104). London: Home Office.

Hanmer, J. and Griffiths, S. (2001) 'Effective policing.' In J. Taylor-Browne (ed.) *What Works in Reducing Domestic Violence? A Comprehensive Guide for Professionals.* London: Whiting and Birch.

Healey, K. and Smith, C., with O'Sullivan, C. (1998) *Batterer Intervention: Program Approaches and Criminal Justice Strategies.* Washington, DC: National Institute of Justice.

Home Office (1990) *Circular 60/1990: Domestic Violence.* London: Home Office.

Home Office (1995) *Inter-agency Circular: Inter-agency Co-ordination to Tackle Domestic Violence.* London: Home Office.

Home Office (2000) *Circular 19/2000: Domestic Violence.* London: Home Office.

Kaufman, K., Barber, M., Mosher, H. and Carter, M. (2002) 'Reconceptualizing child sexual abuse as a public health concern.' In P. Schewe (ed.) *Preventing Violence in Relationships: Interventions across the Life Span.* Washington, DC: American Psychological Association.

Kelly, L. and Humphreys, C. (2001) 'Supporting women and children in their communities: Outreach and advocacy approaches to domestic violence.' In J. Taylor-Browne (ed.) *What Works in Reducing Domestic Violence? A Comprehensive Guide for Professionals.* London: Whiting and Birch.

Levison, D. and Harwin, N. (2001) 'Accommodation provision.' In J. Taylor-Browne (ed.) *What Works in Reducing Domestic Violence? A Comprehensive Guide for Professionals.* London: Whiting and Birch.

Lloyd, S., Farrell, G. and Pease, K. (1994) *Preventing Repeated Domestic Violence: A Demonstration Project on Merseyside* (Police Research Group Crime Prevention Series Paper 49). London: Home Office.

Low, S., Monarch, N., Hartman, S. and Markman, H. (2002) 'Recent therapeutic advances in the prevention of domestic violence.' In P. Schewe (ed.) *Preventing Violence in Relationships: Interventions across the Life Span.* Washington, DC: American Psychological Association.

Mama, A. (1996) *The Hidden Struggle: Statutory and Voluntary Sector Responses to Violence against Black Women in the Home.* London: Whiting and Birch.

McGee, R., Wolfe, D. and Wilson, S. (1997) 'Multiple maltreatment experiences and adolescent behaviour problems: Adolescents' perspectives.' *Development and Psychopathology 9,* 131–149.

Mirrlees-Black, C. (1999) *Domestic Violence: Findings from a New British Crime Survey Self-Completion Questionnaire* (Home Office Research Study 191). London: Home Office.

Mirrlees-Black, C., Mayhew, P. and Percy, A. (1996) *The 1996 British Crime Survey, England and Wales* (Home Office Statistical Bulletin 19/96). London: Home Office.

Morley, R. and Mullender, A. (1994) *Preventing Domestic Violence to Women* (Police Research Group Crime Prevention Series Paper 48). London: Home Office.

Mullender, A. (1994) 'School-based work: Education for prevention.' In A. Mullender and R. Morley (eds) *Children Living wth Domestic Violence: Putting Men's Abuse of Women on the Child Care Agenda*. London: Whiting and Birch.

Mullender, A. (2001) 'Meeting the needs of children.' In J. Taylor-Browne (ed.) *What Works in Reducing Domestic Violence? A Comprehensive Guide for Professionals*. London: Whiting and Birch.

Mullender, A. and Burton, S. (2001) 'Dealing with perpetrators.' In J. Taylor-Browne (ed.) *What Works in Reducing Domestic Violence? A Comprehensive Guide for Professionals*. London: Whiting and Birch.

Mullins, A., McCluskey, J. and Taylor-Browne, J. (2000) *Challenging the Rural Idyll: Children and Families speak out about Life in Rural England in the 21st Century*. London: NCH/The Countryside Agency.

National Campaign against Violence and Crime (NCAVAC) Unit (1998) *Ending Domestic Violence? Programs for Perpetrators. Summary Volume*. Canberra, Australia: NCAVAC Unit, Attorney-General's Department.

Plotnikoff, J. and Woolfson, R. (1998) *Policing Domestic Violence: Effective Organisational Structures* (Police Research Series Paper 100). London: Home Office.

Rai, D.K. and Thiara, R.K. (1997) *Redefining Spaces: The Needs of Black Women and Children in Refuge Support Services and Black Workers in Women's Aid*. Bristol: WAFE.

RESPECT (2000) *Statement of Principles and Minimum Standards of Practice*. Obtainable from DVIP, PO Box 2838, London W6 9ZE.

Short, L.M., Hadley, S.M. and Bates, B. (2002) 'Assessing the success of the WomenKind Program: An integrated model of 24-hour health care response to domestic violence.' *Women and Health 25*, 2–3, 100–119.

Smith, L. (1989) *Domestic Violence: An Overview of the Literature* (Home Office Research Study 107). London: Home Office.

Stanko, E., Crisp, D., Hale, C. and Lucraft, H. (1998) *Counting the Costs: Estimating the Impact of Domestic Violence in the London Borough of Hackney*. Swindon: Crime Concern.

Walby, S. and Myhill, A. (2001) 'Assessing and managing risk.' In J. Taylor-Browne (ed.) *What Works in Reducing Domestic Violence? A Comprehensive Guide for Professionals*. London: Whiting and Birch.

Young, M.E., Nosek, M.A., Howland, C.A., Chanpong, G. and Rintala, D.H. (1997) 'Prevalence of abuse of women with physical disabilities.' *Archives of Physical Medicine and Rehabilitation 12*, Suppl. 5, S34–S38.

Zorza, J. (1995) 'Mandatory arrest for domestic violence.' *Criminal Justice* (Fall), 2–54.

CHAPTER 6

Evidence-Based Practice in Young People's Substance Misuse Services

Paul Keeling, Karen Kibblewhite and Zoë Smith

Until recently there has been relatively little attention given to evidence of effectiveness in interventions for young people with issues around substance misuse. It is known, however, that over the past ten years there have been significant developments in the field of substance use in relation to young people, and over the last five years in particular there has been recognition by government and policy-makers of the importance of targeted service provision for *vulnerable* children and young people concerning substance use. In this chapter we intend to examine what is known about the effectiveness of interventions for young people in relation to substance misuse. In this context, 'young person' is defined as someone under the age of 19, in line with the usage of the government's Drugs Strategy Directorate.

Background: Patterns, trends and prevalence

A growing body of research into young people and substance use has been undertaken in the UK. Much of this has centred on epidemiological studies, which have provided information on the prevalence and incidence of drug and alcohol use amongst the general population of young people, and also amongst specific groups of vulnerable young people. More recently, all Drug Action Teams (DATs) have been required to submit specific plans, and provide subsequent annual updates, for curbing and treating young people's substance use – including alcohol use – in their areas (Drug Prevention

Advisory Service (DPAS) 2001). Part of the process for this includes a needs assessment, detailing numbers of young people known to be using and at risk of using substances.

Key findings from research on young people's substance use can be summarised as follows:

- There has been an unprecedented and continued rise in the number of children and young people using substances.

- It should be recognised that most children and young people who use substances will do so without encountering long-term or significant harm, though even one drug-taking episode may cause significant harm.

- Most children and young people will naturally reach a point of reduction or abstinence in drug taking, and a point of reduction and stability in alcohol use, as part of a wider maturation and development process.

- Some children and young people, however, will encounter problematic patterns of substance use either in adolescence or in adulthood.

- There has been a growth in interest and research activity in risk-group analysis, to identify groups of children and young people who are more likely in the future to develop problematic patterns of substance use; who are currently over-represented in groups of young substance users; and who have already become adult problematic substance users.

While epidemiological data gathered in the UK in relation to young people and drug use show some local variations, overall trends in use can be identified. The percentage of young people who have tried an illegal drug has shown a steady rise since the late 1980s, reaching a peak a decade later and declining more recently for all but cocaine and heroin use. However, the UK still has the highest rate of reported drug use amongst young people in Europe (Plant 2001), and the ages at which young people first try tobacco, alcohol and drugs are falling. Surveys variously report that between 21 per cent and 40 per cent of young people aged 14–16 have tried an illegal drug (Balding 2000; Miller and Plant 1996). Thirty-nine per cent of the young people surveyed by Balding (2000) reported knowing where to obtain illegal drugs and over half (58%) reported knowing a drug user.

A national survey of secondary schoolchildren aged 11–15 indicated that the proportion of pupils who had used drugs in the last month increased from 7 per cent in 1998 to 9 per cent in 2000. The proportion who had used drugs in the last year increased from 11 per cent to 14 per cent over the same period (National Centre for Social Research and the National Foundation for Educational Research 2001). Age at first use does seem to be decreasing, with the percentage of 12–13-year-olds who had tried drugs in 1996 being higher than the percentage of 15–16-year-olds who had tried in 1987 (Balding 1998). Table 6.1 shows the results of a recent survey in terms of the percentage of young people of different ages reporting using various substances.

By the age of 12–13 years, 2 per cent of boys and 1 per cent of girls report having been out of control at some point after taking a drug or drugs, figures which increase to 8 per cent for both boys and girls by the age of 15–16 (Kibblewhite 2002).

It is arguably 'hard' drugs (Class A for legal purposes) that create the greatest social harm, and this is increasingly reflected in government strategy. The British Crime Survey reported that over a fifth of young people aged 16–19 years had used Class A drugs in their lifetime, although the proportions consuming in the last year (8%) and last month (5%) were considerably lower (Kershaw *et al.* 2001). A survey by the polling organisation MORI in 2001, undertaken with 5263 13–16-year-olds in school, found that 3 per cent reported having taken heroin, and 3 per cent reported having taken cocaine (Kibblewhite 2002).

It is the reduction in the age at which young people first start experimenting with substances (including alcohol and tobacco) that is particularly noteworthy. The earlier young people begin using substances, the greater the deleterious effects are likely to be in their late adolescence and early adult life, as substance use often affects education, the ability to make and sustain relationships, social skills, and physical and mental health (Kibblewhite 2002).

Table 6.1 Percentage of young people who have ever used a drug, by age and sex

Drugs	11–12 years		12–13 years		13–14 years		14–15 years		15–16 years	
	Boys	Girls	Boys	Girls	Boys	Girls	Boys	Girls	Boys	Girls
Cannabis	2	1	5	3	12	11	21	24	31	25
Ecstasy	<1	<1	1	<1	1	1	2	2	5	4
LSD	1	1	<1	<1	1	1	4	3	4	4
Amphetamines	<1	<1	1	1	1	1	4	3	4	4
Magic mushrooms	1	<1	2	1	3	2	5	2	5	2
Cocaine	1	1	2	1	1	1	3	2	4	3
Heroin	1	<1	1	<1	1	1	2	1	2	1
Barbiturates	1	<1	1	1	1	1	1	2	2	2
Glue/solvents	7	6	6	7	9	10	9	11	7	9

© Health Advisory Service (from *The Substance of Young Needs* (2001), cited in Beinart *et al.* 2002).

There are a number of methodological problems with the self-report studies often used to gauge prevalence. Some of the limitations include: insensitivity to subgroups beyond the basic demographics of age and sex; the likelihood that some young people with substance-use problems will be excluded from surveys because they are not at school when the survey is administered; and the possibility that young people may be unwilling to disclose their substance use because of fear of punishment or negative labelling. These factors should be taken into consideration when using the results of self-report surveys.

The growth in the body of knowledge that profiles the using behaviours of young people has not been mirrored in the analysis of those factors which play key roles in differentiating those young people who use and those who do not. The importance of risk factors is being stressed increasingly and their use in targeting work is growing in prominence, particularly around the issue of vulnerability. The need also to develop a body of knowledge about those factors which may protect young people from drug use is also recognised, although the study of protective factors remains in its infancy.

Vulnerability to substance use

It is important to be clear about what we mean by vulnerability to substance use. The following definition is the one we use here: 'Vulnerability to substance misuse is the presence in an individual of one or more factors, which may have an influence in them developing a drug problem' (Drugscope and DPAS 2001). Since the prevalence of substance use amongst children and young people is very high in the UK, there is a sense in which the major risk factor for substance use is simply being a young person. However, there are clearly different types of substance use, which have different associated levels of harm, arising both from the nature of the substance being used (e.g. the risks of volatile substances are greater than those of cannabis) and from the method and purpose of use (e.g. moderate weekend social drinking is less risky than heavy binge drinking where the aim is to induce a state of stupor rather than to enhance pleasure and sociability).

The second Health Advisory Service report on substance-use services for young people (2001) recommended that all children and young people in the following groups should be screened for substance use, as they are considered to have greater vulnerability to substance use than the general population of young people:

- young offenders at first contact, with repeated screening at intervals throughout the period of contact

- all receiving mental health assessments

- runaways and 'street' or homeless children

- all those in the 'looked-after' system or in any contact with social services

- those with educational problems, which might be signalled by significant changes in performance and grade or by absences from school

- school 'drop-outs' and those excluded from school

- those with substantial and recurrent disruptive behavioural problems

- those with recurrent contact in accident-and-emergency departments or primary care for trauma-, drug- or alcohol-related incidents

- any child or young person presenting with family conflict or disruption

- any child or young person whose behaviour shows a significant change

- children of parents who may be misusing substances (alcohol and drugs)

- children presenting to accident-and-emergency departments and other services with incidents of deliberate self-harm.

Many young people could potentially fall into one or more of the groups listed above, and this should prompt a note of caution: the presence of one or more risk factors does not automatically mean that the child or young person will experience a substance-use problem. Indeed, one of the main dangers of using risk group analysis is the creation of 'false positives', whereby some young people are stigmatised as being likely to encounter a substance-use problem, or interventions will be inappropriately targeted.

Figure 6.1 summarises what is known about actuarial risk factors for problem substance use among young people.

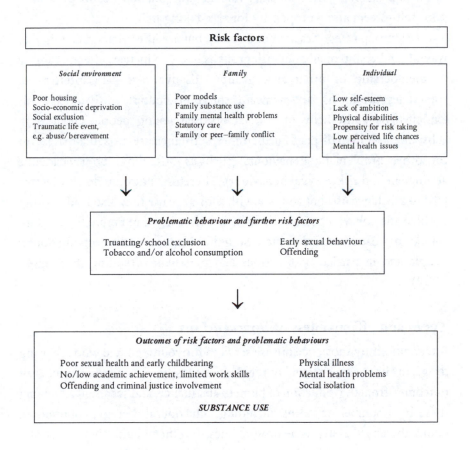

Figure 6.1 The cumulative effects of risk factors and problematic behaviours. Adapted from Kibblewhite 2002.

Social environment risk factors refer to young people's experiences of social relationships and their interactions with their local environment and culture. These include immediate traumatic events as well as the more general disadvantages associated with growing up in a socially and economically deprived area. Family risk factors relate to those young people who are subject to unhelpful influences beyond their control within their family and/or their immediate friendship group. Individual risk factors relate to young people with underlying psychological, social and physical features which are located within the individual, though they are influenced by environmental factors. These include, for example, mental health problems, poor self-esteem and a propensity for risk-taking behaviour.

Risk group categories are not discrete, but are interrelated in a range of ways. Membership of any one risk group is likely to increase the probability of membership of other risk groups; disadvantages are interlinked, sometimes producing a downward spiral of multiple difficulties. This explains the multiplicity of risk factors that young people engaged in substance use often display. Furthermore, substance use is itself a risk factor for other problematic behaviours (such as offending, poor academic attainment and risky sexual behaviour). Therefore, not only do risk factors lead to substance use, but coupled with substance use they also lead to other problematic behaviours. Indeed, the risk factors listed in Figure 6.1 are very similar to those identified as increasing the risk of offending among young people and in particular of serious and persistent offending (Farrington 2002).

Types and effectiveness of interventions

Interventions by substance misuse services for young people who are using drugs, in either experimental or regular patterns, work towards a number of outcomes, from the reduction of harm to abstinence, and set about achieving these by a number of means, including behavioural therapy, counselling, family therapy, 12-step-type programmes, and therapeutic community and residential treatment programmes. In terms of reviewing the effectiveness of each there is little published material on UK programmes. Much of what is known about the effectiveness of various interventions comes from the United States.

The dominance of the USA over the UK in the English language literature is apparent in reviews of available research, for example in the systematic review undertaken for the Scottish Executive by Elliot *et al.*

(2001). While we cannot simply assume that what works in the USA will work here, this review does provide an indication of the potential effectiveness of different programmes. Elliot *et al.* cite evidence that 12-step programmes can be effective in reducing drug use among young people, that behaviour therapy is more effective than non-behavioural approaches, and that cognitive–behavioural approaches are more effective than counselling. Within the UK, 12-step programmes have not been a favoured model, with much more emphasis being placed on community development programmes (Health Advisory Service 2001). Counselling that is culturally sensitive, however, can show promising results, as can family therapy, which out-performed purely educational approaches, individual counselling and group therapy. There is weaker evidence for the effectiveness of school-based programmes, although some aspects of these may be helpful, including skills development, building self-esteem and confidence, and the involvement of parents. Purely educational programmes were found to be generally ineffective in reducing drug use and also in helping with psychological problems (such as depression) and problems in social relationships (such as family problems and offending). Generally, approaches that combine a range of interventions and are able to involve family members seem to do better than programmes that depend on a single method and which focus on the young person in isolation from their social context. These findings are echoed in the review of research by the Health Advisory Service (2001). Elliot *et al.* (2001) conclude (pp.83–84) that it is important to target specific groups for different types of intervention, particularly on the basis of risk, and that the most successful programmes are well funded, carefully planned and long term.

A tiered model of service intervention

The theme of interventions based on risk is fundamental to two important recent documents that outline frameworks for good practice with young people on substance-use issues. In September 2001 the Health Advisory Service published its second report on *The Substance of Young Needs*. This updates and reviews changes in policy, commissioning, the design and delivery of services, and our knowledge of the effectiveness of prevention and treatment interventions since 1996. A number of action steps required to develop an effective approach are highlighted in the report and are listed below. Workers in the field should:

- promote public awareness of substance use and misuse

- develop, disseminate and implement evidence-based education and prevention programmes

- promote and improve the screening and assessment of substance use and misuse in children and young people

- develop, disseminate and implement evidence-based interventions

- ensure equality of access to services for all racial/ethnic and disadvantaged socio-economic groups

- develop and implement a tiered model of services (see Table 6.2)

- develop and implement a plan of integration within existing children's services.

The earlier report (Health Advisory Service 1996) recommended a four-tiered model of service intervention, which, though widely accepted, has not yet been fully implemented nationally. Since 1996 there have been major changes in services for young people, including Youth Offending Teams coming on stream, and the development of the Connexions Service. These are reflected in the 2001 report's model of service intervention.

Table 6.2 A tiered model of service intervention	
Examples of interventions	*Practitioners/agencies*
Tier 1 services (for all young people): providing substance misuse education, information and referral to support services.	
• Information/education concerning tobacco, alcohol and drugs within the education curriculum • Educational assessment and support to maintain in school • Identification of risk issues • General medical services/routine health screening and advice on health risks/hepatitis B vaccination/ referral/parental support and advice	Teacher Youth worker School health/pastoral
Tier 2 services (for young people who may be vulnerable): providing drug-related prevention and targeted education, advice and appropriate support for those identified as at risk of developing problems with substance misuse, *in addition to Tier 1*.	
• Programme of activities and education to address offending • Family support regarding parenting and general management issues • Assessment of risk and protection issues • Counselling/addressing lifestyle issues • Educational assessment	YOT/bail support Social service Counselling One-stop-shop service
Tier 3 services (for young people who are problem drug users): providing specialist (mainly non-medical) drug services and other specialist services that work with complex cases requiring multidisciplinary work, including GPs and other primary care workers.	
• Specialist assessment leading to a planned package of care and treatment, augmenting that already provided by Tiers 1 and 2 and integrated with them • Specialist substance-specific inteventions including mental health issues • Family assessment and involvement • Inter-agency planning and communication	Specialist young people's drug and alcohol services integrated with community mental health services or 'one stop shops' combined with child mental health, educational assessment and support, Statement of Special Educational Needs

Continued on next page...

. . . Table 6.2 continued

Examples of interventions	Practitioners / agencies
Tier 4 services providing very specialist (medical) forms of intervention for young drug users with complex care needs. Services may include specialist residential and mental health teams.	
• Short period of accommodation if in crisis • In-patient/day psychiatric or secure unit to assist detoxification if required • Continued Tier 3 and multi-agency involvement alongside Tier 1 and Tier 2	Forensic child and adolescent psychiatry Social services Continued involvement from YP substance misuse services Substantial support for educations

Adapted from Health Advisory Service 2001.

The tiered model conceptualises the relationship between these levels of prevention and intervention as a pyramid. At the base are Tier 1 services intended to provide a universal and generic service from which all young people will potentially benefit. Tier 2 consists of services for young people provided by workers who have some knowledge and awareness of substance misuse issues but are specialists in working with young people in general rather than specifically with young people who are misusing substances. Tier 3 is aimed at young people who have developed problems with drugs or alcohol and therefore require specialist intervention by substance misuse experts. The final tier consists of highly specialised services, including in-patient treatment and residential care, and is aimed at a very small minority, that is, at those young people for whom substance misuse has become a serious and potentially dangerous problem, whether that danger is to themselves or to others.

The tiered model should allow for the targeting of services on the basis of assessed needs and risks, which the evidence on effectiveness suggests is crucial to the delivery of successful services. It provides a framework that can help to ensure that young people receive the type of service that most closely matches the severity of their substance misuse problems and the damage that they do, while avoiding the risk of negative labelling of young people without serious problems, through their unnecessary involvement in the network of services. In the process the wastefulness of providing specialist services to those who do not need them can be avoided; for example, there is no need for an arrest referral worker from a substance-misuse service to be called to a police station when there is no evidence of a drugs problem, but the young person has been detected as having used cannabis recreationally in the past.

An example of appropriate service provision that avoids stigmatising its recipients is detached and outreach work by substance-misuse specialist workers. Detached work is a style of work based on youth working principles. The worker meets young people on their own ground – in pubs, amusement arcades, parks, and most commonly on the street. The basis of the work is in accepting young people as they are, not because they have been labelled or described as 'disadvantaged', 'delinquent' or 'truant'. Workers do not have to manage or be responsible for a building, allowing them to be more flexible, responsive and responsible to the young people they meet. Outreach work is an extension of work linked to a base, such as a youth centre or a specific young people's drugs project, and can be used to encourage young people to make use of existing provision. It aims to reach young people in the name of the centre or project, and in some circumstances it will bring young people back to the base, developing work with them there. In both varieties of work the aim in connection with substance misuse should be to engage young people's interest sufficiently to allow for relevant and focused information to be given and discussed on sexual health, mental health, careers and general life skills. Workers often 'signpost' young people and accompany them into services. An example of a successful substance-misuse-specific outreach service is described below, together with other examples of useful practice.

Useful practice: Case studies

There is no simple service description to cover the resources that have emerged in the UK to provide interventions for young people in relation to drug use. Many have been established to address identified need and have subsequently grown organically, others are placed within existing services and take forms directly related to funding, while others are a result of partnership working. We outline a few examples below in an attempt to display the range of services being provided and the ways in which they are structured.

An example of a successful approach to young people's substance misuse, which provides a specialist service but is well integrated with other systems and organisations, is to be found in a recently established young people's service in Greater Manchester. The service is supported by and located in the same building as the local Connexions service. The Youth Offending Team also occupies the same building. The service is staffed by trained substance-misuse workers with a social work or health care background, and offers day-care programmes and a range of services graded according to need and risk, from low-threshold advice and information to more intensive one-to-one counselling grounded in cognitive–behavioural approaches. It can be accessed by all young people, agency workers, parents or carers, and any other person seeking advice, information, consultation or support concerning substance misuse by young people. The service has succeeded in attracting a substantial number of the relevant client group and in maintaining contact with them, and its links with other agencies allow for progression into further education or work, or when necessary for expert input into decisions in the youth justice system. The service thus straddles Tiers 2 and 3. Its own intensive work on assessment and behavioural change is an example of Tier 3 provision, while its links with Connexions and the Youth Offending Team fulfil the Tier 2 remit.

An example of a multi-agency approach is a team operating in a borough of Lancashire in which professionals from a range of agencies and services (the Youth Offending Team, education, social services, and health) who are trained in substance misuse interventions come together to provide a net of support services. A number of interventions are offered to young people based on a 'lifestyle' approach: that is, on assessment which looks at a range of risk factors which might lead young people to substance use, and aims to intervene with relevant factors to reduce existing substance use and prevent use in the future. The approach looks at general health, mental health, education, living arrangements, offending behaviour and so on, and can refer young people on to a wide range of other agencies as well as work with them within the service. The importance of multi-agency teams is recognised across a wide range of initiatives. Youth Offending Teams are themselves an example of the multi-agency approach, since they bring together the police, youth justice workers, probation officers, teachers, health professionals and specialist substance-misuse workers (Newburn 2002). The aims of the approach are to improve access to relevant services, including specialist provision, and to promote among practitioners a common sense of purpose and a shared understanding of the nature of the problems locally. The approach requires members of the team to work co-operatively and with respect for each other's perspective, which is not always easy – different agencies may have different agendas, different professionals have different working assumptions, and there may be imbalances of power among the participants (Crawford 1997). But if these difficulties can be overcome the approach promises important advantages in policy coherence, economy and efficiency.

An example of a focused and consequently successful outreach approach is the work done by a Greater Manchester young people's substance-misuse service. This is an example of a service providing targeted interventions in the most efficient way possible, working directly with groups of vulnerable young people in their own settings with issues that concern them. The outreach service uses an adapted bus which provides a space to meet and discuss issues with young people in a safe environment. The bus also carries substance-misuse information and has video facilities.

Central to the outreach service's success is its clear aim as an early intervention service. Although the team provides signposting to other young people's services, such as sexual health, and works alongside the youth service, the principal aim is to educate and inform young people about substance misuse. The workers will also use the bus for more intensive one-to-one work for those most in need. The team recognises that there is a limited lifespan to the work done with young people using the bus (around six weeks/sessions), and plans the sessions with the young people accordingly.

Problems associated with delivering young people's substance misuse interventions

In the not-so-distant past many substance-use interventions were based on the presuppositions that young people (a) did not want to experiment with alcohol and drugs, and (b) that if they were already using them, they wanted to stop. This was a somewhat erroneous assumption. In the light of mounting evidence, services and interventions recognised the reality that increasing numbers of young people experiment with and regularly use substances and that this is becoming increasingly normalised behaviour (Parker *et al.* 1998). Parallels have been drawn with alcohol, the use of which for many stabilises after a period of experimentation which may involve excessive use. The majority of young people do not develop problematic use of either alcohol or drugs.

To try to prevent all young people from taking drugs when they do not want to be prevented from doing so, and in the majority of cases will not experience any long-term harm from substance use, would seem to be a poor use of resources. The focus might instead be better placed on young people who will develop problematic use, concentrating on reducing their risk and vulnerability and on preventing an escalation of substance use from recreational experimentation to problematic use. The moves made by central and local government and, indeed, by many young people's services themselves to mainstream substance-use provision are an initial step toward looking at substance use within the wider context of a young person's life. It is the risk and protective factors present in young people's family and social environments which (largely) determine that fine line between experimental/recreational and problematic use.

Substance use and services for children

It would seem that the main policy focus for substance misuse prevention work should be the mainstreaming of funding to work towards the wider context of addressing risk factors. There has been a considered shift over the past couple of years towards linking children and young people's specialist substance-use provision into mainstream children's services and commissioning. The message from central government is that instead of adapting an adult substance-use service to meet children's needs in regard to substance use, we should look to adapt children's services to meet children's substance-use-related needs. This is reflected in the key message from the second Health Advisory Service report (2001), which is that substance-use services for young people should be incorporated into existing children's services, and indeed this echoes the young people's substance misuse guidance issued by Drugscope and DPAS (2001), which considers the integration of substance-use services into children's services as crucial to their development.

The Department of Health's consultation on planning for children's services in 2000 showed wide agreement amongst local authority and health commissioners that there were too many plans for children and that there was insufficient coherence between them. The Social Services Inspectorate and Department of Health report on *Coordinated Service Planning for Vulnerable Children and Young People in England* (2001) provides a framework in which to locate children's planning, and incorporates two key points:

1. that planning services for children and young people need to involve not only the young people, but also their families, the local authority, statutory and voluntary agencies

2. that service planning should concentrate on vulnerable children.

Recent changes in government policy and requirements on local authorities and Primary Care Trusts reflect the wider mainstreaming of all children and young people's provision; the main themes are outlined below:

- *Children's Trusts* will enable local partners (including social services, health, education and housing) to jointly plan, commission, finance and deliver services for children, and are designed to meet individual needs, rather than being centred on organisational structures.

- *Children's Preventative Strategies* were produced by all local authorities in April 2003. These overarching strategies set priorities for collectively agreed preventive work, underpinned by mechanisms for: performance management and assessment; the mapping of children and families' needs; the identification, referral and tracking of children exposed to risk factors; and key interventions for families and children exposed to risk factors.

- The *Identification, Referral and Tracking Project* (later renamed the *Information Sharing and Assessment Project*) aims to ensure that every child at risk will be identified and if necessary referred to appropriate preventive services, and that their progress will be tracked to ensure that they do not subsequently 'fall through the net'. All local authorities were required to develop integrated systems for identification, referral and tracking by September 2003.

- The *Children's Taskforce* was established in October 2000 to support policy-making and implementation of the NHS Plan. It encompasses health, social care and public-health policy for children, and provides a link for cross-government action on issues concerning children and families.

- Finally, the *Children's National Service Framework* is intended to develop national standards across the NHS and social services for children (including maternity services), and the first set of standards, for maternity services, was issued in December 2003.

These changes all move toward one outcome – the placement of substance-use-specific services within the wider children and young people's commissioning arena. Substance-use services for young people are becoming less substance-use-oriented and more young-person-oriented. Substance use is increasingly understood within the wider context of a young person's lifestyle and behaviours, which allows for working with the variety of risk factors that interplay in young people's lives and the development of 'joined-up' solutions, rather than services and interventions which are issue-specific.

There is a myriad of government-led initiatives aimed at vulnerable young people that have been launched in recent years: Sure Start, the Children's Fund, On Track (for young people at risk of delinquency), and so forth, providing wider support for young people who experience vulnerability to all kinds of problematic behaviours and deprivation. It is important that these initiatives should consistently concern themselves at a local level with issues of substance misuse, and specialist practitioners have an obligation to ensure that they do.

The substance misuse field has changed significantly over recent years and continues to grow and evolve. Workers in the field increasingly recognise the need to develop provision that is guided by principles of quality and effectiveness, and the benefits of doing so. However, for young people's drug services, the providers of interventions and the commissioners of those services must also recognise the need to locate services and interventions within broader structures of service provision. The risk factors for drug use among young people are also risk factors for a range of other problematic behaviours, which interact and evolve into other behaviour sets. Risk and protective factor analysis warrants greater attention, and more needs to be done to understand these factors and their interaction and to develop work based on this understanding. Equally important is developing and disseminating knowledge about effective interventions in the British context. The goal must be to identify risk and design appropriate responses at all tiers of provision, while ensuring that substance misuse services remain in the mainstream of services for children and young people.

References

Balding, J. (1998) *Young People and Illegal Drugs in 1998.* Exeter: Schools Health Education Unit.

Balding, J. (2000) *Young People and Illegal Drugs into 2000.* Exeter: Schools Health Education Unit.

Beinart, S., Anderson, B., Lee, S. and Utting, D. (2002) *Youth at Risk?* London: Communities that Care.

Crawford, A. (1997) *The Local Governance of Crime: Appeals to Community and Partnerships.* Oxford: Clarendon Press.

Drugscope and DPAS (2001) *Assessing Local Need: Planning Services for Young People. Drugs Prevention Advisory Service* (2001). Written communication to Drug Action Teams in England.

Elliot, L., Orr, L., Watson, L. and Jackson, A. (2001) *Drug Treatment Services for Young People: A Systematic Review of Effectiveness and Legal Framework.* Edinburgh: Scottish Executive Effective Interventions Unit.

Farrington, D.P. (2002) 'Developmental criminology and risk-focused prevention.' In M. Maguire, R. Morgan and R. Reiner (eds) *The Oxford Handbook of Criminology.* Oxford: Oxford University Press.

Health Advisory Service (1996) *The Substance of Young Needs – Children and Young People's Substance Misuse Services.* London: HMSO.

Health Advisory Service (2001) *The Substance of Young Needs.* London: Stationery Office.

Kershaw, C., Chivite-Matthews, N., Thomas, C. and Aust, R. (2001) *The 2001 British Crime Survey: First Results, England and Wales* (Home Office Statistical Bulletin 18/01). London: Home Office.

Kibblewhite, K. (2002) *Risk and Response: Prevention and Interventions in Young People's Substance Misuse.* Lifeline: Manchester (unpublished).

Miller, P. and Plant, M. (1996) 'Drinking, smoking, and illicit drug use among 15 and 16 year olds in the United Kingdom.' *British Medical Journal 313*, 394–397.

MORI (2001) *Youth Survey 2001 for the Youth Justice Board.* London: Youth Justice Board.

National Centre for Social Research and the National Foundation for Educational Research (2001) *Smoking, Drinking and Drug Use among Young People in England in 2000.* London: Office of National Statistics.

Newburn, T. (2002) 'Young people, crime and youth justice.' In M. Maguire, R. Morgan and R. Reiner (eds) *The Oxford Handbook of Criminology.* Oxford: Oxford University Press.

Parker, H., Aldridge, J. and Measham, F. (1998) *Illegal Leisure: The Normalization of Adolescent Recreational Drug Use.* London: Routledge.

Plant, M. (2001) *The 2001 ESPAD Report (European School Survey Project on Alcohol and Other Drugs): Alcohol and Other Drug Use among Students in 30 European Countries.* Stockholm: Swedish Council for Information on Alcohol and other Drugs.

Social Services Inspectorate and Department of Health (2001) *Coordinated Service Planning for Vulnerable Children and Young People in England.* London: Department of Health.

CHAPTER 7

Social Work and Looked-After Children

Claire Taylor

Introduction

According to the most recent government figures for England, nearly 59,000 children and young people are in local authority care, representing 0.5 per cent of the total under-18 population (Department of Health 2001a). Trends reveal that the number of children entering care is in decline, but that those already in care are staying longer. Given that the average child in care costs social services £435 a week (Department of Health 2000), which amounts to over £25.5 million a week for the total care population, the vast volume of literature and research on various aspects of care seems to be justified. What is worrying, however, is that while certain themes have been swamped by research, other areas remain comparatively neglected.

One topic that has received surprisingly little attention from child care researchers and criminologists is the relationship between experiences of care and criminal behaviour. The disproportionate number of young offenders who have been in local authority care is evident year after year from the prison statistics, and is now generally regarded as a criminological given. About 38 per cent of the young prisoner population have spent a period in care (Frost and Stein 1995), compared to about 2 per cent of the general population. The story is a familiar one, but there has been no real attempt to explain it – just a simple acceptance among academics and child care professionals alike. What is of central importance, and has never been seriously addressed, is how we can avoid assuming that looked-after children will *necessarily*, *inevitably* and *obviously* fare worse and achieve less than all other young people.

In this chapter I focus on the link between care and criminal careers, drawing on insights from my doctoral research, which examined this topic in some depth. Based on qualitative interviews with young people who had been looked after, the research aimed to explore the diversity of care experiences as well as the different pathways that young people may take between care and custody. After a brief outline of the research methods employed, I report some of the key findings of the study, focusing particularly on protective and risk factors associated with various aspects of care. I finish by considering the implications of the research, with particular reference to the messages for social work practitioners working with looked-after children.

Research questions and methods

Although it is recognised that some young people do enter care as known offenders or with a 'baggage of disadvantage', the research set out to explore how going into care might counter the effects of previous negative family experiences, and protect against subsequent offending behaviour. The following themes and questions were at the heart of the study:

- We should not accept the relationship between care and criminal careers without question, but should seek to consider how care might be made a more positive experience. Which aspects of the care experience might promote social inclusion, and help to reduce the disproportionate number of care leavers who become part of the prison population?

- Low expectations of looked-after children, among policy-makers, social workers and carers alike, can lead to a self-fulfilling prophecy if young people feel that there is little point in trying to achieve. Often such expectations have exacerbated the problems already faced by young people and reinforced the likelihood that they will face social exclusion in the future. Yet a consistent finding throughout the literature is that, even with prolonged negative early experiences, there is a very marked heterogeneity of outcomes (Rutter *et al.* 1998). What are the mechanisms involved that enable certain individuals to be resilient in the face of previous psychosocial adversity?

As well as questioning the link between care and criminal behaviour, a further aim of the research was to give a voice to young people with first-hand experience of the care system. It was hoped that their voices would enable both positive and negative aspects of care to be identified. Qualitative interviews with young people who had been looked after were regarded as the best method for addressing the research questions and aims. In order to consider aspects of the care experience that may be protective against offending behaviour, I chose to explore the experiences of both care leavers who had been in custody and care leavers who had not.

In 1999 and 2000 I interviewed 39 young people who had been looked after, half of whom were in prison custody at the time of the interview. Fifteen of the interviewees were male and 24 female. Their ages ranged from 16 to 27, with a median age of 18. Interviewees were accessed from various locations in the south-east and north-west of England. Young people interviewed outside of custody (n=19, 14 of whom were female) were initially identified through leaving care schemes and then through a snowball sampling strategy. The 20 young people interviewed in custody were identified with the help of probation and prison officers in two young offender institutions, and were split evenly between males and females.

Interviews were intended to be semi-structured and to allow for in-depth exploration of care experiences, enabling the young people to tell their own stories of how the care experience had affected their lives. Issues of confidentiality and anonymity were addressed at the beginning of each interview, when it was also made clear that the participants would be asked to discuss only issues with which they felt comfortable. All interviewees were assured that there would be no record of the interview that included their name, and that all names would be changed in the dissemination of the research results. The majority of the interviews were tape-recorded, with the consent of the young person, and the Atlas/ti computer package was used to code and analyse the data produced.

The diversity of care careers

One of the first things to become abundantly clear in the project was that there is a very diverse range of care careers. Among the young people I interviewed, some had chosen to go into care themselves, some were placed in care through the criminal justice system, some were placed by civil courts, and some by their families. Certain individuals experienced only foster care or only residential provision, but many experienced both. Some interviewees had been in multiple placements whereas others had been in just one. The youngest age of reception into care was three, the oldest 17.

Some young people spent a considerable amount of time moving back and forth between different care placements and their own homes. Others never returned home after being placed into care. Some young people welcomed going into care, others hated the fact that they were in care, and still others felt that as it was the only life they had ever known they could not really compare it with anything else.

The key point is that popular perceptions that tend to lump all young people in care together are very misleading, and ignore the range of different routes that individuals may take through the care system. The common labelling of children in care as mad or bad (Morris 2000) results from a failure to appreciate the actual diversity of care experiences. This lack of understanding is reflected not only in public assumptions about the care system, but also in policy and practice. A common complaint from interviewees about social services was their failure to provide care on an individualised basis; instead, everybody was treated in the same way, regardless of their needs. As one interviewee commented:

> I didn't feel it was personalised for me enough. I kept thinking I've been through different things from all the other kids I've met. Why am I being treated the same? (Melanie, aged 20)

Mayhem in residential care

Within the wide diversity of care careers, there were inevitably some recurrent themes in the experiences described by the young people. Key findings emerged in relation to particular types of care provision. With regard to life in residential care, many interviewees painted an incredibly bleak and depressing picture. It is important to note that some positive experiences of children's homes were reported and that foster care was not appropriate for everyone. However, positive experiences were few and far between when compared to the mayhem and misery experienced by many young people in residential settings.

> The police were there every day, it was ridiculous... We had a six-year-old little girl running round with plastic knives and forks trying to stab people. Kids getting up on the roof, setting the fire alarm off, just totally destructive. (Beth, aged 19)

> We'd climb out in the middle of the night and run wild. We'd all sniff gas in the back garden or get pissed and come back effing and blinding. We'd get done for breach of the peace. Stupid things really. (Gemma, aged 18)

Of the 31 young people who had been in residential care, 23 spoke of getting into trouble, becoming involved in offending behaviour, or absconding during their time in a children's home. Eleven of these 23 reported having been in trouble with the police prior to their admission to care, but the evident potential of a residential setting to promote delinquency is still disturbing.

For those who had already been involved in offending, going into care seemed to have little effect in terms of reducing their involvement in criminal behaviour. Rather, for young men in particular, their criminal behaviour appeared to escalate. Donnie (19) had twice been cautioned by the police before going into care at the age of 14. He had been in and out of jail since the age of 17.

> Basically I got all my criminal convictions from when I was in care and from when I left care... When I went into care, you went in and you had to like be with the high people...people who were like top dogs or whatever... I was just going out and getting into trouble with everyone else, getting in trouble with assault charges, theft charges, burglary charges and all kinds of stuff... I just went straight downhill.

Liam (26) also noted that his anti-social behaviour had escalated after he entered residential care at the age of 12:

> When I went into care it sort of stepped up a level. There was a lot of peer pressure and that. You know you might not want to do something, but if

everyone's there you've got two choices, get in trouble with the people you live with or get in trouble with the staff. And if you're living with people you've got to get on with them, so it's an easier life going out and getting arrested, because then you're all right in their eyes, you know, they trust you.

Worryingly, even those who had never previously been in trouble spoke of being introduced to various delinquent activities once in the care system. Sinclair and Gibbs (1998) found that 40 per cent of young people with no cautions or convictions prior to entering care (n = 674) acquired one during their time in a children's home. Indeed, residential child care has often been referred to as a socialising milieu for delinquency (Stewart *et al.* 1994), and this was clearly reflected in the stories of several of the young people in this study.

Gemma (18), who went into care when she was three, felt very strongly that she would not have ended up in prison were it not that she had been in care nearly all her life:

> Because I wouldn't be mixing with the environment what I was mixing with in care…going out robbing people, taking drugs and that, sniffing gas and that. I didn't have a clue about any of that until the kids' homes. People showed me things like that and I didn't have a clue.

Interestingly, two other young women reported having left their children's homes with criminal records as a result of assaults on staff. Both suggested that the staff might have been over-zealous in their reactions. Tracy (16) had never been in trouble with the police before going into care at 15, yet she left residential care with two convictions for assault. She described one assault on a member of staff, for which she received a fine:

> I was messing about in the kitchen…and I wouldn't get down off the side, I was looking for something… And I just got down and I was like in a hyper mood and I pushed the door to get out the way and it just hit her on the shoulder… She took me to court.

Donna (16) was particularly bitter about the assault charges she had received:

> My criminal record is through care, for assaulting staff. I've got nowt else on my record apart from one charge… If I'd have flicked me fingers and it accidentally caught them it was assault, do you know what I mean?

Of course these accounts give only the young people's interpretation of events, but their stories illuminate an important aspect of life in residential care. O'Neill (2001) recently noted that many local authorities have a policy of reporting to the police any young people who caused 'criminal damage' in residential units (cf. Carlen 1987). This may be another factor in explaining why so many young people leave residential care with a criminal record.

Stories of life in residential care frequently included references to bullying, self-harming and a perceived couldn't-care-less attitude on the part of disillusioned staff. These all emerged as important risk factors associated with offending behaviour. However, regardless of the different reasons that young people put forward for their involvement in crime, one striking theme that emerged in many of their stories was that there was always a crowd to follow. In other words, a consistently deviant subculture already existed in the residential homes, which meant that new residents were introduced at least to the possibility of delinquency. The experiences of many of the young people interviewed highlight that institutionalised adolescents continue to be heavily influenced by their peers (cf. Polsky 1962).

The findings of this study certainly confirm that, as is well known, criminal behaviour can lead to an admission to care, but they also show that the relationship can work the other way round. Certain types of care career, particularly those associated with the worst features of life in a residential setting, can intensify, create and promote criminal behaviour.

Having someone who cares

Conversely, certain types of care career, particularly those that provide stability, security and a quality relationship with carers, can protect against offending behaviour. Having someone who cared emerged as a highly significant theme in this respect. Among those who had been involved in crime, many spoke of feeling that nobody cared about them once they had been placed in care. In turn, they had nobody to be bothered about and were free to behave as they wished. This was a particularly common finding among those who had been in residential care, where a lack of staff continuity frequently contributed to the residents' feeling that nobody really knew what was happening in their lives.

> The people that ran the actual children's home, they were always swapping over, so we never got a chance to speak to anyone about anything, or, if we did, they wouldn't be there any more. The next person who came along wasn't clued up enough to know what was happening in our lives. (Jackie, aged 18)

In contrast, foster care seemed to offer more potential for carers and young people to get to know each other. Ten interviewees were identified as having developed secure attachments with their foster carers. Such attachments tended to develop in the context of long-term foster placements (although the placements were not always originally intended to be long term).

At the age of seven Carol (27) went with her sister into a foster placement that was intended to last for 6 weeks. Carol ended up staying for 13 years and taking her carers' surname as her own.

> It was nice to be treated as a family… We just sort of felt really comfortable, you know you was always made to feel comfortable. And after the years it was 'Oh, you look like your Dad', and it's like 'That's not my real Dad', you know, it was really funny.

Jenny (18) also developed a quality relationship with her carers:

> My carer was the number one person for me, got on really, really, really well…both the mum and the dad, I just took them on as my parents really… You know, anything that we wanted to do, they'd come with us and support us, like doctors, dentist, anything silly like that they'd be there for us.

Among those who were lucky enough to experience care as a secure base and to develop strong attachments, there was a general feeling that going into care had been a positive turning point in their lives.

> Had we not been placed with Lynn, I dunno what would have happened to us…It did us a favour going into care 'cos of what our life was like before. I'd probably have ended up like my mother, pregnant at sixteen and into drugs. (Louise, aged 26)

Helen (18) told a story that placed her foster carer firmly at the centre of the achievements of Helen's life:

Helen: If I was still living at home I wouldn't have a job, I wouldn't have gone to college, I wouldn't have got through school, I wouldn't have done all of them.

Claire: So what has it been about the care system, what's changed?

Helen: Well, it's more the foster parents really. I mean Trish took me into her home and treated me as one of her own kids, which made me trust people... She's one in a million, she is...she's just like a second mum really.

It is well documented that various protective mechanisms can enable young people to overcome previous psychosocial adversity (Rutter *et al.* 1998). One particular mechanism that may enable resilience is that which opens up new opportunities and turning points in life (Howe *et al.* 1999). The stories above indicate that, for some young people, the care experience can act as a very positive turning point. As Helen's story suggests, the development of quality relationships with carers tends to be a crucial aspect of this turning point.

An additional protective mechanism that has been identified in the literature on resilience involves the promotion of self-esteem through the development of secure and supportive relationships. High self-esteem tends to develop most strongly within the context of secure and supportive relationships (Howe *et al.* 1999). In the current study it was very noticeable that those who had developed a secure attachment in care were most likely to have a positive self-image: 'It's built up my self-esteem, my confidence. I'm just a totally different person. I could talk to you for hours' (Sarah, aged 17).

The stories of those who had developed secure attachments in the context of care also highlighted the crucial importance of being sensitive to and caring about the opinion of others (Hirschi 1969). Having respect for a carer and not wanting to let them down were identified as important aspects of the care experience that could protect against involvement in crime, or prevent further offending. Just three of the ten securely attached individuals had been in trouble with the police, whereas none of those interviewed in custody were identified as securely attached.

Many interviewees (23 out of 39) pointed out that it was easy to break the rules in care and get into trouble if you wanted to. When some of the securely attached young people were asked what would stop them from breaking the rules, respect for carers emerged as a common theme.

> I always thought that I didn't want to disrespect her. (Helen, aged 18)

> It's really important to find the right foster carer for kids… Respect for my carers would stop me getting into trouble, but if you don't have respect then you don't care. (Laura, aged 19)

Although Laura's first foster placement broke down, her second one was very positive and she developed a quality relationship with her carer: 'I came to realise it's not so bad being good… When I did have a good placement I didn't fight, I didn't want to. I didn't have any reason to.'

Developing secure attachments to carers can enable resilience to previous psychosocial adversity. However, in order for such relationships to develop, certain care conditions need to be in place. In particular, young people need to experience care as a secure and stable base. By exploring the experiences of those who had developed secure attachments with their carers, this study highlighted that, contrary to commonsensical assumptions, some care experiences can in fact be very positive.

Implications for policy and practice

In the year ending September 2000, data on the offending rates of looked-after children were gathered for the first time (Department of Health 2001b). The figures revealed that looked-after children of the age of criminal responsibility are three times more likely to be cautioned or convicted for an offence than their peers. Of children looked after for more than a year, 10.8 per cent received a caution or conviction, compared with 3.6 per cent for all children (Department of Health 2001b).

Following the publication of these figures (which was some time after the research discussed above had been completed), the Department of Health established a target, developed under the 'Quality Protects' programme (see Department of Health 1998), for the reduction of offending by looked-after children.

> By 2004, the proportion of children aged 10–17 and looked after continuously for at least a year, who have received a final warning or conviction, should be reduced by one-third from the September 2000 position. This sets a target to reduce the proportion from 10.8% to 7.2%. (Department of Health 2001c)

Social work practitioners will inevitably be one group of professionals in the front line of efforts to meet what looks set to be a challenging target. In the remainder of this chapter I consider what messages they might take from the summary of research results reported above.

First, the research has highlighted the need to respond to looked-after children as individuals. This requires recognition of both the diverse range of experiences that young people in care bring with them and the variety of pathways that they may take through the care system. Recognising and promoting the individuality of young people in care requires an in-depth understanding of their histories and experiences. It also involves appreciating that what is appropriate for one person may not be appropriate for everyone. Practitioners and carers need to take a flexible approach in order to ensure that individual needs are fully met, rather than adopting a 'one size fits all' strategy. Young people emphasised that they did not want to be viewed or treated as 'children's home kids' or 'care kids', but rather as individuals in their own right.

On a related note, it is very unhelpful to regard looked-after children as 'damaged', as this implies that they are beyond help or repair. It is much more useful to regard them as vulnerable, and acknowledge that it is possible to make individuals less susceptible to vulnerability by promoting the notion of resilience (Gilligan 2001). This may result in higher expectations of looked-after children, and consequently in better outcomes in adulthood.

Of particular importance is that the research findings are definitely not interpreted as part of a debate on residential care versus foster care. The themes of the research happen to have resulted in an emphasis on some of the best aspects of foster care and the worst aspects of residential care. However, it was evident from the young people's accounts that we need both types of provision. Although there is a tendency to see residential provision as the poor relation of foster care, both need to be regarded as potentially positive options. The 'last resort' mentality associated with residential care must be replaced with more ambitious aims and objectives for residents and carers, so that both groups are valued.

The stories of young people support the view that residential care experiences may be enhanced when units are smaller. Smaller units can provide more individualised care for children, and may reduce the likelihood that residents will develop and maintain a deviant subculture. The power of peer pressure is also likely to be reduced when there are fewer peers to pressurise.

Other commentators have noted the advantages of smaller units (e.g. Frost *et al.* 1999), and recent government figures indicate that 50 per cent of residential homes now accommodate six or fewer residents (Department of Health 2001d). But worryingly, the same figures reveal that there are still 101 homes that can accommodate more than 13 residents, and an additional 142 homes that can accommodate 10 to 12. There is undoubtedly a need for the government to make a concerted effort to reduce the capacity of as many of the larger units as possible.

In addition, policy-makers and practitioners should aim to promote staff continuity in the residential sector. This may be a more achievable goal in smaller homes, and fewer residents will need fewer staff. It is extremely difficult for young people to get to know their carers, and indeed feel that they have someone to talk to, when staff are constantly coming and going. However, if smaller staff groups worked more regularly in the same home, there would be more opportunities for staff and young people at least to get to know one another, and potentially establish some trust and respect. Young people in care need to have someone that they can turn to, and the importance of feeling that someone actually cares cannot be emphasised enough.

It is noteworthy that for young people resident in homes that are characterised by a high staff turnover, the social worker's role may be absolutely crucial in providing some much-needed continuity in the young person's life. By the same token, in long-term foster placements where young people have developed quality relationships with their carers, the social worker's role may fade into the background.

A further implication of the research presented here is that the potentially positive benefits of long-term foster care ought to have more recognition. Although it is not appropriate for everyone, the study demonstrated that long-term foster care provides the most realistic opportunity for young people to develop secure attachments with their carers. On a related note, the experiences of the young people interviewed also provide support for Minty's (1999) claim that the current policy of short-term admissions to care may not always be in the child's best interests. This is because it can encourage the 'oscillation' of children in and out of care, with the result that some long-term admissions are simply postponed.

Finally, in order to improve outcomes for looked-after children who offend, there is a real need for inter-agency co-operation between child care and youth justice workers. What would be the most efficient way for these agencies to share information so that looked-after children who offend do not become lost in the criminal justice system? Making youth justice workers aware of the 'looked after' status of relevant young offenders could certainly help to highlight the vulnerability of these individuals.

Furthermore, practitioners need to be aware of the policy of some local authorities to report to the police any children who cause criminal damage in residential homes or assault members of staff, and how far this impacts upon the overall offending rate of looked-after children. While residential care staff cannot be expected to put up with abuse from children, it may well be worth exploring what actually constitutes 'assault' and 'criminal damage' in local authority homes.

Of course, we know that some young people have a history of offending prior to their admission to care. However, we may be drawing some looked-after children into the criminal justice system unnecessarily because of routine local authority policy. It could, on the other hand, be argued that such a policy is justifiable in that it serves to protect residential care staff. Such questions warrant exploration in order to further our understanding of the link between care and criminal careers.

Conclusion

This chapter has focused on the relationship between experiences of care and criminal behaviour, and considered how the offending rates of looked-after children could be reduced. Drawing on research findings from a qualitative interview study of formerly looked-after young people, it has argued that certain types of care career can intensify and/or create delinquency. On a more optimistic note, certain types of care career can be very positive for some individuals, and can help to protect against involvement in crime. There is much to be learned from the stories of young people who feel that care has had a positive impact on their lives. The very existence of these individuals means that there is absolutely no reason to assume that the outcomes for looked-after children will inevitably and obviously be poor.

References

Carlen, P. (1987) 'Out of care, into custody.' In P. Carlen and A. Worrall (eds) *Gender, Crime and Justice.* Milton Keynes: Open University Press.

Department of Health (1998) *Quality Protects – Transforming Children's Services.* London: Department of Health.

Department of Health (2000) *Children in Need in England: First Results of a Survey of Activity and Expenditure as Reported by Local Authorities Social Services' Children and Families Teams for a Survey Week in February 2000.* London: Department of Health.

Department of Health (2001a) *Children Looked After in England: 2000/2001* (Statistical Bulletin 2001/26). London: Department of Health.

Department of Health (2001b) *Outcome Indicators for Looked After Children: Year Ending 30 September 2000.* London: Department of Health.

Department of Health (2001c) 'Reducing offending among looked after children.' At www.doh.gov.uk/qualityprotects/work_pro/project_16.shtml (accessed June 2004).

Department of Health (2001d) *Children's Homes at 31 March 2000, England* (Statistical Bulletin 2001/9). London: Department of Health.

Frost, N., Mills, S. and Stein, M. (1999) *Understanding Residential Care.* Aldershot: Ashgate.

Frost, N. and Stein, M. (1995) *Working with Young People Leaving Care: A Training and Resource Pack.* London: HMSO.

Gilligan, R. (2001) *Promoting Resilience: A Resource Guide on Working with Children in the Care System.* London: BAAF.

Hirschi, T. (1969) *Causes of Delinquency.* Berkeley: University of California Press.

Howe, D., Brandon, M., Hinings, D. and Schofield, G. (1999) *Attachment Theory, Child Maltreatment and Family Support: A Practice and Assessment Model.* London: Macmillan.

Minty, B. (1999) 'Annotation: Outcomes in long-term foster family care.' *Journal of Child Psychology and Psychiatry 40,* 7, 991–999.

Morris, J. (2000) *Having Someone who Cares? Barriers to Change in the Public Care of Children.* London: National Children's Bureau.

O'Neill, T. (2001) *Children in Secure Accommodation: A Gendered Exploration of Locked Institutional Care for Children in Trouble.* London: Jessica Kingsley Publishers.

Polsky, H. (1962) *Cottage Six.* New York: Sage.

Rutter, M., Giller, H. and Hagell, A. (1998) *Antisocial Behaviour by Young People.* Cambridge: Cambridge University Press.

Sinclair, I. and Gibbs, I. (1998) *Children's Homes: A Study in Diversity.* Chichester: Wiley.

Stewart, J., Smith, D. and Stewart, G., with Fullwood, C. (1994) *Understanding Offending Behaviour.* Harlow: Longman.

CHAPTER 8

Practice for What?

The Use of Evidence in Social Work
with Disabled People

Bob Sapey

In setting out to evaluate the evidence for what is effective in social work practice with disabled people, I want to ask two questions: (1) is it is possible to determine what evidence there is for effective practice without first gaining agreement on what the aims of providing social work services are? and (2) how should such evidence be produced – by disabled people, social workers or academic researchers? My hope is that in trying to answer these questions I will be able both to explore critically some of the evidence that does exist and simultaneously to remain sceptical about whether evidence-based practice is an appropriate approach to this work.

What are the aims of intervention?

Over the past 40 years there has been a revolution in our understanding of disability, and in the more recent past there have been some significant changes in the aims of social welfare in respect of disabled people. The importance of the social model of disability has led to the development of disability studies internationally, and academics and activists in the field have been strong critics of current welfare structures. In practice it is only in the very recent past that UK governments have begun to change the way in which care is delivered by the state and then only with permissive legislation. Contrasting the analysis of welfare by disabled people with the responses of the state will give some indication of the need to ask this first question.

The social model of disability developed out of the experiences of disabled people, particularly from the social and economic segregation caused by the fact of welfare being provided through residential and nursing care. When the Union of Physically Impaired Against Segregation (UPIAS) was formed in the early 1970s, its members began to redefine disability as the oppression resulting from a social response to impairment rather than as the effect of impairment itself. This position argued for a different under-standing of the causal relationships that led to impaired people being disabled. In their opening statement to the Disability Alliance at a meeting in 1975, UPIAS made clear how this position would have to lead to changes in professional practice within the welfare state:

> ...disability is a situation, caused by social conditions, which requires for its elimination, (a) that no one aspect such as incomes, mobility or institutions is treated in isolation, (b) that disabled people should, with the advice and help of others, assume control over their own lives, and (c) that professionals, experts and others who seek to help must be committed to promoting such control by disabled people. (UPIAS 1975, p.4)

At that time the main piece of community care legislation relating to disability, the Chronically Sick and Disabled Persons Act 1970, was in its infancy. Rather than seeking to allow disabled people to have control over their lives, this Act made it clear that it was for the local authority to decide whether or not individuals had a need for a prescribed list of services – a regulatory approach which was described by Middleton (1992) as being akin to an MOT test. When services were provided they would be designed and delivered by professionals with little reference to the views of the people for whom they were being provided (unless the individual social worker chose to seek them) and with no reference at all to the views of representa-tive organisations such as UPIAS. Indeed, it would have been organisations *for* rather than *of* disabled people that could have had most influence, as some, for example the Spastics Society (now renamed Scope) and the Leonard Cheshire Foundation, were providing a substantial number of services.

These organisations were providing very institutional services, as illustrated by the discussion Tobias (1968) had on the ethical and practical issues involved in marriage and disabled people. In the debates and questions that had arisen within the Spastics Society in the course of their deliberations over whether to provide accommodation for couples, the main ethical dilemma for the professionals was whether the organisation would be acting responsibly to encourage marriage between disabled people. This clearly reflected the paternalistic attitudes that were governing social work with disabled people, but, on the other hand, the fact that the debate was taking place also signified a time at which attitudes were beginning to change, albeit sluggishly, owing to the conservatism of the professionals.

During the past two decades the sophistication of the social model analysis has developed but the rate of corresponding change in practice has remained slow. From 1982 to 1993 there was a significant growth in spending on social welfare, but this was almost entirely confined to residential care via the social security system. However, one positive development to arise from the creation of the Social Fund in 1988 was the setting up of the Independent Living Fund, through which disabled people were able to gain control over their own personal assistance needs and provision. This level of control is now available through the direct payments schemes being operated by many local authorities. However, in an inspection of ten English councils, the Social Services Inspectorate (2000) said that, although independent living had become a reality for a few younger disabled people, primarily through direct payments and other creative schemes, the majority were

> …still being offered services in a fragmented way without any obvious consideration of whether they will promote independence. (para. 1.1)

Returning to the original question, I would ask whether the aims of local authorities have ever included the promotion of independence in the sense that UPIAS would have understood it, as autonomy and control – or whether they remain concerned with independence as a purely functional issue, that is, that disabled people should be able to undertake personal care tasks without assistance. It may be that from this traditional, functional perspective the services being provided do not appear to be fragmented. If this is so, then the extent of the differences between disabled people and the institutions of state welfare is considerable, and this emphasises the importance of first agreeing the aims of intervention. One of the more significant studies of the outcomes of community care to have taken place was conducted by Priestley in the 1990s. He argued that service purchasers should re-evaluate their ideas of quality to help people achieve equality of citizenship. He says that reaching

> ...any level of social consensus about the validity of such an approach is prob-
> lematic, since it poses a direct challenge to traditional ways of thinking about
> disability and welfare. As an approach to quality, it extends far beyond the ad-
> ministrative confines of 'community care' to issues of inclusion, citizenship,
> equality and participation in the wider world. If outcome measures are con-
> sidered in this context then there are enormous implications for the design of
> services aimed at achieving them. (Priestley 1999, p.189)

Achieving this type of change will require a significant shift in the way local authorities work in partnership with disabled people. Priestley also draws attention to government concern that local authorities' failure to collaborate with service users results in inappropriate outcomes:

> ...the experience of the service user can be too easily overlooked. Again and
> again we found definitions of QA [quality assurance] in use and evidence of
> standard setting which overwhelmingly represented the views of managers
> and professionals rather than those of the service user. (Department of Health,
> cited in Priestley 1999, p.139)

So, on the one hand, we have traditional, institutional services which aim to provide those assessed as needing help with the minimal functional support they need to be safe. On the other hand we have disabled people who wish to receive services that will enable them to take control of their lives, that will help them gain access to mainstream economic and social life and hence to gain equality of citizenship. The Association of Directors of Social Services (1999) indicates that it is committed to disabled people taking control of services through direct payments but, while its own survey of English local authorities (ADSS 2000) is up-beat about the progress made, it also shows that three-quarters of these authorities had fewer than 20 people receiving direct payments three years after the scheme's implementation.

This, along with the fragmentation described by the Social Services Inspectorate, would suggest that, locally, directors are not as committed to the aim of independence as their national association claims.

The issue for evidence-based practice is this: While these aims remain disputed, what evidence should social workers attempt to use? Clearly, the answer to this will depend on whether social workers follow the guidance of their employers, which in the case of local authorities may be in direct conflict with the aspirations of those citizens most affected – disabled people.

Who can produce the evidence?

Within the debates about the validity of evidence-based practice there is some criticism of the dominance of behavioural research. Webb (2001), for example, points to the ways in which such approaches are used in conjunction with managerial agendas to technologise the provision of social work. Sheldon (2001) counters this by alleging that the real conspiracy is the exclusion of behaviourism from social work education. He questions this anti-behaviourism and asks whether its proponents would be quite so opposed to it in relation to the education of dentists or pilots. However, the need to argue the case for behaviourism in social work by looking outside at more 'scientific' occupations is only convincing if we suspend our knowledge about the real nature of social work. We should ask why it is necessary to seek examples from dentistry or aviation rather than from social work itself because, if social work does lend itself to this level of certainty, why does Sheldon need to go outside the field to make his case?

While social work academics, managers and practitioners may argue about the value of the certainty that comes with behaviourism within their occupational activities, the research agenda of disabled people themselves has been concerned with more fundamental questions about the production of knowledge. Oliver (1992) argued that it was necessary to move beyond both the positivist and interpretivist paradigms within which research had traditionally been conducted, to what he termed an 'emancipatory paradigm':

> [E]xisting research paradigms have proved inadequate and hence, will not be useful in trying to construct a disability research agenda for the future. Issues highlighted by disabled people...can only be tackled by building a new research paradigm which fundamentally changes the existing social relations of research production. (p.113)

His concern was that research had constructed false knowledge of disability. While proponents of the traditional paradigms were arguing about issues of the reliability and validity of the various approaches to studying what they saw as problems of disability, disabled people themselves were most often excluded from the process and therefore were unable to contribute to defining the problems that required further understanding. The development of the social model of disability pointed to disability as a political problem, and for Oliver it was necessary for disabled people to take control of the research agenda for this view to become dominant in knowledge production.

Some years earlier Finkelstein (1980) had argued that the way in which psychological understandings of disability had been constructed was not through listening to the experiences of disabled people or even through positivist studies of them as benign subjects, but through non-disabled psychologists imagining what it would be like to be impaired. This simulation approach has also been used in social work training, but its flaw lies in its exclusion of those who experience the reality of impairment and disability. Instead, simulation tends to draw on the fears people may have of something they have not experienced, and usually fails to replicate the structural oppressions that are actually present in the real lives of disabled people.

In research terms the effect of the exclusion of disabled people, and hence the need for a political perspective within disability research, were very clearly illustrated by Oliver's development of alternative questions to those used by the Office of Population Censuses and Surveys (OPCS) in the 1986 disability surveys.

- OPCS question:

  Have you attended a special school because of a long-term health problem or disability?

- Alternative question:

  Have you attended a special school because of your education authority's policy of sending people with your health problem or disability to such places?

- OPCS question:

  Does your health problem/disability mean that you need to live with relatives or someone else who can help look after you?

- Alternative question:

  Are community services so poor that you need to rely on relatives or someone else to provide you with the right level of personal assistance?

(Adapted from Oliver 1992, p.104.)

There are two significant issues in these alternative questions. First, the answers that would be gained would be about the failings of institutions rather than of individuals; and, second, they would be unlikely to reinforce negative feelings that people may already have had imposed on them. The knowledge about disability to be gained thus would be about the effects of people being structurally oppressed because they have an impairment, rather than having as its basis the assumption that the impairment is the cause of any disadvantage disabled people may face. The difference in approach is perhaps best summarised in Oliver's alternative to the first question of this survey: 'Can you tell me what is wrong with you?' becomes 'Can you tell me what is wrong with society?'

The politicisation of disability gives rise to an analysis of the power relations that exist not only within the care industry in terms of the design and delivery of services, but also within the production of knowledge that informs their practices. Just as UPIAS had said that 'disabled people should…assume control over their own lives, and…professionals, experts and others who seek to help must be committed to promoting such control', the emancipatory paradigm of research was promoting control of the research agenda and process by disabled people. Barnes (2003) argues that

> [i]n contrast to traditional investigative approaches, the emancipatory disability research agenda warrants the generation and production of meaningful and accessible knowledge about the various structures: economic, political, cultural and environmental, that created and sustain the multiple deprivations encountered by the overwhelming majority of disabled people and their families. (p.6)

While disabled people need to be in charge, research could include non-disabled people. Morris (1992), while supporting the principle of disabled people taking control of the research agenda, argued that non-disabled researchers could be allies. They would, however, need to question both the absence of disabled people within most research and their own attitudes towards disability. This would need to result in

> [t]urning the spotlight on the oppressors. Non-disabled people's behaviour towards disabled people is a social problem…because it is an expression of prejudice. Such expressions…take place within personal relationships as well as through social, economic and political institutions and, for example, a study of a caring relationship therefore needs to concern itself with prejudice… (p.165)

So, to try to answer the question of who can produce the evidence: from a social model perspective it may well involve non-disabled people – but as allies to a research agenda controlled by disabled people. As with the question about the aims of intervention, it is possible for those with power – for example, local authority social workers – to ignore this social model analysis and to concentrate on the production of evidence to support their functional approach to providing services; but this would set them in opposition to the people they purport to be helping, thereby contributing to the problem of disability. Social workers need to be able to distinguish between evidence produced to support the interests of those with power and evidence aimed at empowering disabled people, and for this it is important to be able to recognise the paradigms within which knowledge is produced.

Emancipatory disability research

What exactly would a piece of emancipatory disability research look like? It is unlikely to come with a label attached guaranteeing its pedigree; instead, it is likely to conform to a certain set of ideas and principles which would inform the ways in which it was undertaken. Barnes (2003) suggests there are four areas under which the key characteristics of this model will become clear: the problem of accountability; the social model of disability; choice of methods; and empowerment, dissemination and outcomes.

While Barnes maintains that accountability is essential, he acknowledges that a number of factors combine to make it very difficult to demonstrate. A pure form of emancipatory disability research would probably involve a politically aware organisation *of* disabled people being in full control of the aims of the research, of its conduct and of its dissemination. However, as Barnes points out, there are many researchers with a commitment to using their skills and resources to produce research that might help empower disabled people, although their access to suitable groups as research partners may be restricted. Equally, there are politically active groups of disabled people whose research agendas may be very localised and who are less able to devote energies to supporting academic researchers. Emancipatory disability research may therefore be produced by a variety of people, but seeking accountability to disabled people should remain an essential objective.

The social model of disability is an essential element of good disability research, especially where that may concern professional welfare practice. Barnes makes the point that in the past it may have been difficult to be open about examining disability from this perspective, but that many of the institutions and organisations that once opposed this analysis have now adopted it themselves. Unfortunately, this may not be as true for local authority social work, where the individual model of disability has always been prevalent (Oliver and Sapey 1999). The social model of disability may take a long time to infiltrate the social work orthodoxy, which is based upon a very different understanding of disablement, that of loss:

> Both OTs [occupational therapists] and social workers tended to see impairment in terms of loss and bereavement. People becoming disabled were believed to go through a grieving process for which the practitioner required special skills. Further training in the 'psychology of disability' or loss and bereavement counselling were cited by groups of social workers and OTs respectively as desirable for work with people with disabilities. (Ellis 1993, p.12)

This is complicated by social workers' tendency to confuse social and individual models of disability with social and medical care. Oliver and Sapey (1999) argue that the social model is often misconceived as the horticultural model put forward by Miller and Gwynne (1971). Given the importance being placed on reflective practice, the type of evidence that could be gained by people practising from such a perspective would certainly fail to meet the criteria of emancipatory research. Social workers will need to be cautious of what they use as evidence, as much of it will fall a long way short of the standards being set by disabled people themselves.

Barnes' next issue was around the choice of methods, where he suggests that, although emancipatory disability research has been much more closely associated with qualitative approaches, there is certainly room for numbers as well. The difficulty with quantitative methods is their tendency to be associated with objectivity, which conflicts with one of Oliver's (1992) original points, and is reiterated by Barnes, that for those working in the emancipatory paradigm, 'political commitment and empowerment are the unequivocal aims' (Barnes 2003, p.11).

Given the emphasis on anti-oppressive practice in social work education since the late 1980s, working from an overtly political perspective concerned with emancipation ought not to be a problem. Recently, however, the shift to evidence-based health and social welfare is giving students a mixed message. The Open University, for example, promotes the use of randomised controlled trials as the superior method of research (Gomm 2000), and the guidelines from the Association of Directors of Social Services (1996) seek to retain quantifiable objectivity. The scope for the inclusion of 'political commitment and empowerment' in such designs is negligible, and this puts local authority social workers in something of a dilemma. On the one hand, their employers and some educators are seeking evidence that has been conducted outside this emancipatory paradigm and, on the other, they are expected to practise anti-oppressively, which implies that they should be acting as allies to disabled people within a social model approach. This confusion casts doubt on whether social work should be evidence-based when it involves disabled people.

In Barnes' final area of empowerment, dissemination and outcomes, there are many practical issues that concern how the results of research reach disabled people and also remain within their control so that they can be used to help people empower themselves. Oliver (1992) draws on Freire's work to argue that power cannot be given in this context and that instead it must be *taken* by disabled people. However, within social work it may often be assumed that empowerment is in the gift of the practitioner. For example, recently (the time of writing is July 2002) there was an email discussion by social workers on the subject of 'What is social work?'.[1] While the discussion wandered quite a lot, with no real consensus being attained, one strand that appeared was the call from social workers themselves to be given more power in order that they could then empower others. If this seeking of power is widespread amongst social workers, the gap between their practice and the aspirations of disabled people is likely to be immense, and it raises some fundamental questions about whether social workers should continue to have a role in working with disabled people.

What research matters?

This question of whether disabled people actually need social workers arises, therefore, in part because many of the latter are located in settings where the aims of their employing organisations may be at odds with the aims of true independent living. Social work operates within a political and moral context: political in the sense that decisions hinge on resources, and moral in that judgements about who is deserving are often being made. So, for example, in social work with disabled people a significant proportion of such work concerns gatekeeping resources that people need in order to be able to live independently, but with decisions about allocation being based on the categorisation of need by the local authority. The current care management systems arose because of the need to administer increasing budgets and the simultaneous rise in demand for services, not as a means of improving the outcomes for disabled people. This motivation is illustrated by Lloyd (2000), who points out the increased likelihood of people with Parkinson's disease receiving a community care assessment if there is a carer present – the result of social services' concern to avoid the responsibility for full care falling on them. The aims of policy in relation to this are about administrative control of resources rather than independent living for disabled people.

The moral judgements being made by social workers need to change if their intervention in this field is to become useful. These changes are at many levels, not least at the level of the personal values of the workers themselves. I have argued elsewhere that social workers need to recognise that the primary reason for their involvement

> …is not the individual's impairment, but the ways in which society perceives people with impairments. This is made difficult by both the structure of social welfare agencies and the focus of social policy, in which disabled people are identified, defined and made separate from the rest of society. The task for the social worker will involve overcoming the structural, institutional, cultural, professional and personal barriers that contribute to the problem. However, none of this can be achieved effectively if social workers themselves hold onto an identity that devalues difference and impairment. Social work is an inter-personal activity and it cannot take place effectively if one person in the working relationship believes themselves to be superior to the other. (Sapey 2002, pp.188–189)

Accordingly, in looking at what research may be useful to social work practice with disabled people, it is necessary to consider the following issues. Does the research come from a social model perspective? Does it focus on the causes of disability within contemporary social organisations? Does it help social workers, both disabled and non-disabled ones, to overcome negative attitudes towards impairment?

I want now to look at some of the published material to suggest where such evidence may be found. For five years from 1994 to 1998 I regularly reviewed a number of journals and reports related to social work, and I found 80 studies relating to disabled people. It should be stressed that this review was not an exhaustive one and that it relied to a great extent on what material was sent to me. Nevertheless, I believe that, certainly in relation to disability issues, there were sufficient sources for it to be representative of what was being published in the UK during this period.

The first point of interest is that in the distribution of the disability papers between various journals and publishers, one journal, *Disability & Society*, accounted for over half the published literature. However, this is not a social work journal and perhaps is unlikely to have a very widespread readership within that occupation – it is the leading international disability studies journal and specifically encourages its writers to be clear about the models that inform their research. Just over a fifth of the reports were from the Joseph Rowntree Foundation, which has social care and disability as one of its research priorities. These reports may be more accessible to social workers in that they have sometimes been produced in conjunction with *Community Care* magazine, and summaries of each study appear in full text on *Caredata* at the Electronic Library for Social Care. The research is also governed by a set of principles which would meet the criteria for emancipatory disability research.[2] However, only 10 of the 80 papers were in journals targeted specifically at social workers.

I do not intend to provide a comprehensive review of the disability research literature, as I have explained where it can be found, but I do wish to provide a flavour of what it contains. The research I am describing covers a wide range of issues. In relation to housing, for example, the British Council of Disabled People (1995) has shown the ineffectiveness of the NHS and Community Care Act in improving policy and provision. The Council highlighted ways in which services could be improved, including more collaboration with disabled people and the adoption of the social model by agencies. Heywood (1994) found similar variations in practice in relation to home adaptations and also pointed to examples of good practice that others can follow.

The theme of involving disabled people was picked up by several organisations and individuals as the key to improving services. The Greenwich Association of Disabled People (1994) reported on a project to train disabled people to manage their own personal assistants, and emphasised the importance of disabled people acting as trainers. This of course has much relevance to the use of direct payments. King (1994), while not directly concerned with social work, stressed the importance of disability equality training within agencies wishing to collaborate effectively. It is vitally important to remember that such training also needs to be provided by disabled people, qualified as equality trainers.

Children are considered in various ways in the literature. Bryony Beresford (1996) identified limitations in financial resources and professional help as two areas which were adversely impacting on families with disabled children, while Morris (1997) applied a social model analysis to social work practice and showed how it was resulting in the loss of family life and increased risks of abuse. In relation to adolescence, Tisdall (1994) was very critical of transitional services based on functional independence for the way they created marginalisation, and instead invited professionals to consider citizenship. Keith and Morris (1995) also considered non-disabled children who were being labelled as carers by social welfare agencies because they lived with a disabled parent. They strongly criticised the way in which this was being constructed as a problem. Again, their social model analysis required social workers to re-evaluate their attitudes towards disability at both a personal and institutional level.

The problem of poverty was picked up by Peter Beresford (1996), who challenged the dominant understandings of the causes of poverty and their link to disability. While his was a global analysis, in contrast Noble *et al.* (1997) focused on the relationship between the spread of the Disability Living Allowance and the funding and assessment arrangements established by the NHS and Community Care Act 1990.

The issue of need was picked up by Sim *et al.* (1998), who examined the ways in which different models of disability affect its assessment by disabled and non-disabled people. Other aspects of community care were examined by Morris (1994), who contrasted the experience of disabled people who were able to purchase their own help through the Independent Living Fund with that of people reliant on social services departments. She particularly highlighted the negative impact of the latter and the ways in which such services can be oppressive. Bewley and Glendenning (1994) focused on how local authorities can consult with disabled people, and their work has provided a basis for good practice in this respect. Pilgrim *et al.* (1997) made use of personal accounts to illustrate the way disabled people have experienced both health and social care services, and in doing so they argued that, in a consumerised welfare system, such individual stories provide valuable knowledge for social workers to consider when reflecting on their own practice.

While not specifically related to social work, Reeve's (2000) analysis of oppressive practice by counsellors raised issues that need to be considered by social work practitioners. Her work is in a similar area to that of Thomas (1999), who has extended the social model of disability to include psycho-emotional effects and impairment. Thomas's work is of immense importance to an occupation based on psychosocial methods of intervention, and illustrates the extent to which the social model is an organic idea that is developing.

Also at the level of theory, Begum *et al.* (1994) have attempted to deconstruct the social model literature in relation to ethnicity and race. Their work provided a very important starting point for the inclusion of black perspectives within the social model of disability and was directly targeted at social workers. At a more academic level Priestley (1998) developed a typology which is very helpful to those trying to understand the ways in which the individual and social models affect practice.

Conclusions

Returning to my original questions, it is clear that the promotion of evidence-based practice in the field of social work with disabled people must take account of the politicisation of disability if it is to be effective. To ignore the social model of disability will simply result in social workers and their managers further disabling people while deceiving themselves that they are acting more professionally. This requires a focus on outcomes because, if these are not first agreed with disabled people, there is little point in seeking evidence for effectiveness.

The range of evidence for what is needed to improve the lives of disabled people is broad and has been developing over a long period of time. Hunt's (1966) collection of papers under the title *Stigma: The Experience of Disability*, and the formation of UPIAS shortly after, laid down a challenge for those involved in the segregation of disabled people. With the importance being placed on evidence-based practice today, it is essential that social workers do not allow themselves to be guided by knowledge that sets back the fight for independent living, but rather that they use the evidence of emancipatory disability research to further change and develop services with disabled people.

Effectively, most research into disability issues is taking place within the field of disability studies, which is important to acknowledge if social work practice is to be informed by useful research findings. On this basis the first step for any social work agency that wishes to follow an evidence-based approach to services for disabled people would be to subscribe to *Disability & Society* and to order relevant reports of research being undertaken by the Joseph Rowntree Foundation. This would not be very expensive for such organisations, but would give them access to about three-quarters of the relevant material.

The second step would be for managers to disseminate this knowledge to their staff. However, given the nature of the research within this field, it would be insufficient to leave it at this and expect practitioners to develop and modify their individual work with disabled people. Moreover, much of the evidence from this literature points to the need for institutional change, and it is as important for managers of services to pay attention to their findings as it is for individual practitioners to review their own personal values and practice.

Notes

1.   See archive at www.jiscmail.ac.uk/cgi-bin/wa.exe?A1=ind0206&L=uksocwork.
2.   See www.jrf.org.uk/funding/priorities/scdc.asp.

References

Association of Directors of Social Services (1996) *Guidelines for Researchers Wanting Support from the ADSS Research Group.* Hampshire: Association of Directors of Social Services.

Association of Directors of Social Services (1999) *Response to 'Community Care (Direct Payments) Act 1966 Draft Policy and Practice Guidance Consultation Paper'.* ADSS, available at www.adss.org.uk, July 2002.

Association of Directors of Social Services (2000) *Getting Going On Direct Payments.* ADSS, available at www.adss.org.uk, July 2002.

Barnes, C. (2003) 'What a difference a decade makes: Reflections on doing "emancipatory" disability research.' *Disability & Society 18*, 1, 3–17.

Begum, N., Hill, M. and Stevens, A. (1994) *Reflections: Views of Black Disabled People on their Lives and Community Care.* London: Central Council for Education and Training in Social Work.

Beresford, B. (1996) *The Needs of Disabled Children and their Families – Findings, Social Care Research 76.* York: Joseph Rowntree Foundation.

Beresford, P. (1996) 'Poverty and disabled people: Challenging dominant debates and Policies.' *Disability & Society 11*, 4, 555–567.

Bewley, C. and Glendenning, C. (1994) 'Representing the views of disabled people in community care planning.' *Disability & Society 9*, 3, 301–314.

British Council of Disabled People (1995) *The Effect of Community Care on Housing for Disabled People – Findings, Housing Research 155*. York: Joseph Rowntree Foundation.

Ellis, K. (1993) *Squaring the Circle: User and Carer Participation in Needs Assessment*. York: Joseph Rowntree Foundation.

Finkelstein, V. (1980) *Attitudes and Disabled People: Issues for Discussion*. New York: World Rehabilitation Fund.

Gomm, R. (2000) 'Understanding experimental design.' In R. Gomm and C. Davies (eds) *Using Evidence in Health and Social Care*. London: Sage.

Greenwich Association of Disabled People (1994) *Evaluation of an Independent Living Skills Project – Findings, Social Care Research 48*. York: Joseph Rowntree Foundation.

Heywood, F. (1994) *Adaptations for Disability – Findings, Housing Research 123*. York: Joseph Rowntree Foundation.

Hunt, P. (ed.) (1966) *Stigma: The Experience of Disability*. London: Geoffrey Chapman.

Keith, L. and Morris, J. (1995) 'Easy targets: A disability rights perspective on the children as carers debate.' *Critical Social Policy 44/45*, 36–57.

King, C. (1994) *Development and Training for Self-Organised Groups of Disabled People – Findings, Social Care Research 45*. York: Joseph Rowntree Foundation.

Lloyd, M. (2000) 'Where has all the care management gone? The challenge of Parkinson's disease to the health and social care interface.' *British Journal of Social Work 30*, 737–754.

Middleton, L. (1992) *Children First: Working with Children and Disability*. Birmingham: Venture Press.

Miller, E. and Gwynne, G. (1971) *A Life Apart*. London: Tavistock.

Morris, J. (1992) 'Personal and political: A feminist perspective on researching physical disability.' *Disability, Handicap & Society 7*, 2, 157–166.

Morris, J. (1994) 'Community care or independent living.' *Critical Social Policy 40*, 24–25.

Morris, J. (1997) 'Gone missing? Disabled children living away from their families.' *Disability & Society 12*, 2, 241–258.

Noble, M., Platt, L., Smith, G. and Daly, M. (1997) 'The spread of Disability Living Allowance.' *Disability & Society 12*, 5, 741–751.

Oliver, M. (1992) 'Changing the social relations of research production?' *Disability, Handicap & Society 7*, 2, 101–114.

Oliver, M. and Sapey, B. (1999) *Social Work with Disabled People* (2nd edn). Basingstoke: Macmillan.

Pilgrim, D., Todhunter, C. and Pearson, M. (1997) 'Accounting for disability: Customer feedback or citizen complaints.' *Disability & Society 12*, 1, 3–15.

Priestley, M. (1998) 'Constructions and creations: Idealism, materialism and disability theory.' *Disability & Society 13*, 1, 75–94.

Priestley, M. (1999) *Disability Politics and Community Care*. London: Jessica Kingsley Publishers.

Reeve, D. (2000) 'Oppression within the counselling room.' *Disability & Society 15*, 2, 669–682.

Sapey, B. (2002) 'Physical disability.' In R. Adams, L. Dominelli and M. Payne (eds) *Critical Practice in Social Work*. Basingstoke: Palgrave.

Sheldon, B. (2001) 'Some considerations on the validity of evidence-based practice in social work: A reply to Stephen Webb.' *British Journal of Social Work 31*, 801–809.

Sim, A., Milner, J., Love, J. and Lishman, J. (1998) 'Definitions of need: Can disabled people and care professionals agree?' *Disability & Society 13*, 1, 53–74.

Social Services Inspectorate (2000) *New Directions for Independent Living: Inspection of Independent Living Arrangements for Younger Disabled People*. London: Department of Health.

Thomas, C. (1999) *Female Forms: Experiencing and Understanding Disability*. Buckingham: Open University Press.

Tisdall, E. (1994) 'Why not consider citizenship? A critique of post-school transitional models for young disabled people.' *Disability & Society 9*, 1, 3–17.

Tobias, A. (1968) 'Marriage and handicapped people.' *Case Conference 15*, 6, 218–223.

UPIAS (1975) *Fundamental Principles of Disability*. Disability Archive, University of Leeds, available at www.leeds.ac.uk/disability-studies/archiveuk/archframe.htm, July 2002.

Webb, S. (2001) 'Some considerations on the validity of evidence-based practice in social work.' *British Journal of Social Work 31*, 57–79.

CHAPTER 9

Seven Ways to Misunderstand Evidence-Based Probation

Peter Raynor

The background: 'What works' and the rediscovery of rehabilitation

Recent history's most spectacular example of a wholesale conversion to evidence-based practice can be found in the National Probation Service of England and Wales. Although the Probation Service is no longer regarded by government or by its own senior managers as part of social work, this is a relatively recent development, and it certainly has at least as much in common with the methods and knowledge base of other branches of social work as they have in common with each other. The deliberate change of image, which now emphasises the Service's criminal justice and public protection roles, still encompasses a serious (and arguably increasing) commitment to helping offenders to reduce their offending, and it is here that the majority of evidence-based development has occurred. This is not the place to discuss whether other branches of social work have been, by contrast, reluctant to recognise their regulatory duties and social control functions, and perhaps have more in common with probation services than they realise (Harris 1989). However, at a time when other social work texts (such as Davies 2002) are dropping their probation chapters, it is good to have an opportunity to restate the historical connection and explore what social work might learn from the probation experience.

The story of probation's rediscovery of rehabilitation and of the 'what works' movement, towards evidence-based policy and practice in working with offenders, has been told in more detail in various parts of the criminal justice literature (see, for example, McGuire 1995; Raynor and Vanstone 2002), but the key elements can be summarised quite briefly. During the 1960s and early 1970s the dominant rationale for probation officers' work with offenders was a form of psychodynamic casework theory (see, for example, Hollis 1964) modified to accommodate the fact that probation involved a court order, and thus was not a completely voluntary arrangement on the model of a therapeutic relationship (though in those days it did require the offender's consent). Writers such as Foren and Bailey (1968) explained how, in their view, this apparent contradiction could be resolved by recognising that offenders might not be mature enough to see that probation was good for them, but if they became more mature – perhaps with the probation officer's assistance – they would come to see that supervision had been in their best interests all along, thus giving a kind of notional consent in retrospect and salvaging the important casework principle of voluntarism. There is not space here to explore the subtleties of this somewhat strange argument; it is sufficient to note that, despite difficulties of this kind, probation officers of that time largely identified with the emerging social work profession and shared with other social workers a robust lack of anxiety about the absence of convincing outcome studies to validate their theories and 'practice wisdom'. This was the 'treatment' era in work with offenders: the medical model dominated thinking about rehabilitation, but without the equivalent of medical science to support it.

By the mid-1970s, research had begun to cast serious doubt on the effectiveness of social casework in general (Fischer 1976) and on its specific contribution to reducing offending, whether in a preventive role (Powers and Witmer 1951; Meyer *et al.* 1965) or in a rehabilitative role, seeking to reduce further offending (Lipton *et al.* 1975; Brody 1976). The Probation Service adapted very well to these apparent setbacks: indeed they may have given some support to the Service's tradition of allowing considerable autonomy and freedom to its officers, since if whatever you did was equally likely to be (in)effective, there was little reason for management to interfere with your decisions. The implications of a 'non-treatment' approach were explored (Bottoms and McWilliams 1979; Raynor 1985) and a new, more achievable mission was found in the reduction of custodial sentencing. The provision of 'alternatives to custody' required the Service to influence decisions made by sentencers, which seemed a more feasible task than changing offenders, and still might reduce crime if negative effects of custody could be avoided. By 1984 this was government policy, set out in policy guidance to probation services (Home Office 1984) and even supported by research, at least where juvenile offenders were concerned (Thorpe *et al.* 1980).

By the early 1990s the consensus that 'nothing works' to rehabilitate offenders was being challenged from a number of directions. Practitioners in Britain had begun to develop some learning-theory-based methods of active and practical work with offenders which prefigured the later development of 'programmes' (for example, McGuire and Priestley 1985), while more extensive research in other countries had begun to identify some characteristics of work which was proving to be effective (Andrews *et al.* 1990; Lipsey 1992; Ross and Fabiano 1985). Some relatively successful and adequately evaluated local projects from the 1980s (Raynor 1988; Roberts 1989) were followed by a more systematic pilot of a developed Canadian programme, with modestly encouraging results (Raynor and Vanstone 1996, 1997). Meanwhile the political context was changing rapidly, and not in probation's favour: a largely constructive and liberal Criminal Justice Act in 1991, which promised the Probation Service a 'centre stage' role in reducing reliance on custodial sentencing, was quickly modified, and its central principles were swept away by a sudden lurch into populism orchestrated by an electorally insecure, right-wing government. 'Prison works', proclaimed a new Home Secretary in 1993, and a decade's worth of diversionary policies crumbled into dust. In these circumstances the Probation Service (regularly briefed against by ministers, attacked in the Press, struggling to defend its training arrangements and threatened with effective abolition by merger into the larger Prison Service) needed a new message and a new rationale. Largely through the tireless efforts of the Chief Probation Inspector of the time, the late Sir Graham Smith, opportunities were created to redefine what the Probation Service could offer to the criminal justice system. The principles and methods of evidence-based practice and the new 'what works' research seemed to offer a new foundation for the development of a valued and constructive role.

From the mid-1990s, developments accelerated rapidly. Some key events were: Gill McIvor's review of evidence on effective sentencing for the Scottish Office (McIvor 1990); the first 'What Works' conference in 1991; the launch of the Effective Practice Initiative in 1995, and the publication in the same year of McGuire's edited collection of papers from the 'What Works' conferences (McGuire 1995); the 'Underdown Report' on effective supervision in 1998 (Underdown 1998); the launch of the 'What Works' Pathfinder projects and the Joint Accreditation Panel in 1999; and the launch of the National Probation Service for England and Wales in 2001.

Faced with such rapid changes and such powerful demands that they should alter the way they worked, some practitioners questioned many aspects of the 'what works' movement. A critical literature began to develop out of the concerns of practitioners and sceptical criminologists, and the probation officers' trade union, the National Association of Probation Officers (NAPO), played a key role in this both through its conferences and through the *Probation Journal*. Many of the criticisms are helpful and point to real problems which need to be addressed (for example, Merrington and Stanley 2000), but many also appear to rest to some degree on misunderstandings either of what the available research supports, or of how the new developments are being implemented. Some misunderstandings have acquired a broad currency, and the main purpose of this paper is to explore the debate by considering seven of the more widely repeated concerns, and what evidence might be available to address them. I consider these in three groups: first, concerns which express or inform some practitioners' resistance to the new methods; second, some misunderstandings which seem to flow from a managerialist orientation and seem likely to cause difficulties in the implementation and 'roll-out' of new practices; and finally the nostalgic mythology which argues, impossibly, that it would be better not to change.

Scepticism and resistance

One of the more obvious manifestations of the move towards evidence-based probation has been the widespread introduction of cognitive–behavioural programmes for medium-risk and high-risk offenders ('risk' here means risk of reconviction). This has also led to the first of the critical reactions I want to explore: the belief that programmes are *inherently conser-vative, pathologising individual offenders and ignoring social causes of crime.* This is a widespread concern, spelled out for example in NAPO's policy statement on accredited programmes (NAPO 2002) and by other critics such as Gorman (2001) and Kendall (2002). NAPO refers to both 'a simplistic model of offending that isolates individual behaviour from its social, economic and political context', and 'a medical model which labels people who commit offences'. Certainly, a model which concentrated exclusively on individual responsibility for offending and ignored social context would fit well with a neo-liberal, anti-welfare political stance, but there are many ways in which neither contemporary political realities in Britain nor the criminological assumptions behind evidence-based probation fit such a model. For example, even a cursory examination of instruments developed to assess offenders' needs for rehabilitation, such as the Canadian LSI-R (Andrews and Bonta 1995) or the Home Office's own Offender Assessment System (OASys) (2001), shows that many of the factors taken into account are social and environmental, including various consequences of disadvan-tage. Some authors (such as Hudson 2002) have rightly pointed out that the use of such factors in risk assessments can further disadvantage the poor if the consequences of assessment include greater severity of punishment or longer confinement. However, where such instruments are appropriately used to support rehabilitation, assistance and the least custodial option, this danger is reduced.

As for pathologising offenders, the need for rehabilitative services exists mainly among relatively persistent offenders who persistently get convicted, and it would be perverse to deny that a number of these have difficulties in the areas of self-management, problem-solving and social skills, as well as social disadvantages. The former may derive partly from the latter, and may also contribute to them. Individuals in similar social circumstances may offend differently, and we need to be particularly interested in the character-istics which help to distinguish those who offend to a significant degree from those (the rest of us?) who offend less. A large volume of reputable research has documented the interacting mixture of social and personal characteristics which is associated with significant offending (see, for example, Farrington 2002; Andrews and Bonta 1998), and a recent Home

Office evaluation of resettlement 'pathfinder' services for short-term prisoners suggested that the most effective projects were those which *combined* attention to prisoners' social resources and opportunities with attention to cognitive factors such as beliefs and motivation (Lewis *et al.* 2002).

Those who argue for spending on social programmes instead of on programmes for individual offenders (Kendall 2002) may be setting up a false dichotomy: of course social programmes are needed, but some of them will have their impact on crime in the next generation, when today's children are growing up. In the meantime we need also to be doing something for people who need help now to escape from a pattern of offending. This is often not simply a matter of opportunities but of how and whether they use them. Cognitive–behavioural programmes, being based on social learning theory, assume not so much that offenders are inherently pathological as that they learn in ways which are fundamentally similar to the ways the rest of us learn. It is also an everyday experience that people vary somewhat in the way they learn: they learn different things with different degrees of ease or difficulty, faster or slower, in different styles. To notice this does not imply 'pathologising' or a 'medical model'. The language of 'cognitive deficits' may not be the most elegant way ever devised to describe learning needs, but it is a bizarre misrepresentation to portray it as some kind of Lombrosian search for atavistic 'criminal characteristics'.

A related misunderstanding portrays the process of programme development and accreditation as *dominated by psychologists* and consequently only interested in cognitive–behavioural programmes (Mair 2000). Of the 12 appointed members of the Joint Prisons and Probation Accreditation Panel in 1999–2002 (13 including the Chair), only seven were psychologists, and only one of the seven nominated members was a psychologist. The panel accredited or recognised not only cognitive–behavioural programmes but also 12-step addiction programmes and therapeutic communities. Not all were group programmes: some were for one-to-one use. Eventually new criteria were developed for 'integrated systems' of provision that contained a variety of elements which needed to be combined with appropriate assessment, case management and matching; the first of these to be recognised, Enhanced Community Punishment, contains no conventional 'programme' (though it does use methods such as pro-social modelling), and one of its intended outcomes is an improvement in basic skills to enhance employability. Half of the Probation Service's target number of accredited programme completions are intended to come by this route. The assertion that only cognitive–behavioural programmes are supported is simply a mistake.

A third regularly advanced criticism is that *the 'what works' agenda is indifferent to diversity*; in other words, the particular needs of women or of minority ethnic offenders are likely to be insufficiently recognised by risk assessment methods (Shaw and Hannah-Moffatt 2000) or programme designs (Kendall 2002) which are based on research that has primarily involved white male offenders. NAPO (2002) has also referred to 'potentially discriminatory' content and 'racist and sexist language and assumptions'. It is certainly true that research tends to start where large numbers are available, so that majorities are often studied before minorities, and much the same can be true of programme provision where there are targets to be met. However, it is also clear that the amount of work being done by the Probation Service to try to address diversity issues in effective practice is far more than can be summarised here, and has already included a diversity review of programme content and extensive research on programmes for minority ethnic offenders (Powis and Walmsley 2002). A current project is surveying Black and Asian experiences of probation and 'Pathfinder' projects incorporating different models of specialised provision are under way and being evaluated. Development work is also under way concerning racially motivated offenders (Perry 2002). We do not know how successful this work will be, but the conditions are in place for learning to occur.

More work is also needed in the area of programmes which reflect specific needs of women offenders: some early attempts were not successful in attracting support or accreditation because their good intentions were not matched by convincing programme content, and another design is at the pilot stage. The theoretical basis of such gender-specific provision is also the subject of strongly held positions and active debate, well summarised by Gelsthorpe (2001). Studies of effective practice with women offenders (e.g. Dowden and Andrews 1999) and of risk factors associated with women's offending (Clark and Howden-Windell 2000) suggest some overlap with what we know from research on men, together with some differences reflecting the different circumstances and motivation of some women's offending and the different opportunities open to women in society. It would seem odd to argue that what we learn from men can never have any relevance to women, or indeed vice versa. In a recent Home Office evaluation of risk-need assessment instruments in probation (Raynor *et al.* 2000), the LSI-R (Level of Service Inventory Revised) predicted reconviction almost as accurately for women as for men, but this only means that some of the same risk factors are relevant for both – not that their needs are identical. It was also clear, from this and other studies, that for a given LSI-R score the associated risk of reconviction is lower for a woman than for a man, suggesting a real risk of over-predicting reconviction if the same instruments are applied to both groups without appropriate modification. Overall, the critics who concentrate on diversity issues have helped to ensure that these questions are not ignored or sidelined. The more evidence-based the debate becomes, the more likely it is to lead to real changes.

The fourth and last criticism to be examined in this section is that *the implementation of 'what works' in probation is running too far ahead of the evidence.* This has been carefully argued by Merrington and Stanley (2000), who point out that many of the programmes now being implemented on a large scale have not yet been subject to a full reconviction study. The Accreditation Panel in particular has been aware of conflicting drives – on the one hand, to be sure about the effectiveness of programmes and, on the other, to 'go to scale' as soon as possible where there is judged to be a reasonable amount of evidence. In a context driven by Treasury targets it is not very practical to wait for the necessary three years or so which would be needed for a full reconviction study between the end of every pilot and the decision to implement more widely; this would also slow down another aspect of effectiveness, which is the culture change towards an effectiveness-driven service.

In these circumstances the Panel has reviewed other evidence of the effectiveness of methods used in a programme, and has made quite frequent use of 'recognition' rather than full accreditation ('recognition' enables a programme to be used pending resubmission with fuller evidence within a specified time). In every case the evaluation is in place and the results are being collected, so evaluation and implementation are proceeding side by side, and even full accreditation is reversible, being subject to revision in the light of emerging evidence. An important test of the evidence-based approach over the next three years will be how the Service reacts when some programmes do not produce the expected results. It is to be expected that not everything will work; more time would have been helpful, but was not available. Already the investment in ongoing evaluation has been unprecedented in its scope and thoroughness, and this in itself seems a promising sign for the future.

The perils of management

At this point it seems right to turn, in the interests of fairness and balance as well as thoroughness, to two misunderstandings which seem particularly likely to affect managers, of both the national and local varieties. They can be summed up as the beliefs that *only programmes matter* and *there is a technical fix for everything.*

The first of these, 'only programmes matter', is the same belief that has been criticised by the Chief Probation Inspector as 'programme fetishism' (Her Majesty's Inspectorate of Probation 2002). It consists in an exclusive focus on the delivery of programmes at the expense of other essential elements of practice, such as case management and the maintenance of appropriate contact and communication with offenders under supervision. The origins of this lie partly in the influence of earlier programme delivery practice in the prison system: there the emphasis could primarily be on programmes, as the prisoners were already in prison, being to some degree looked after, and not simultaneously struggling with all the practical problems they would meet in the community. Delivering programmes outside institutions invites very high non-completion rates unless offenders are helped to comply: the case manager's role becomes essential in helping to maintain motivation and commitment, and helping people to deal with problems and challenges which are otherwise likely to disrupt their attendance on programmes and prevent them from benefiting. None of this can be done without contact. It is easy to understand why the early focus of 'what works' was on delivering programmes, since that involved the largest cultural shift in the Service, but case management now needs to become a priority. In some areas, case management seems to mean little more than assessing an offender and assigning him or her to a programme, which is then meant to carry the whole supervision task. In other areas, case management continues throughout the order, and there is at least suggestive evidence that this can mean higher completion rates (Heath *et al.* 2002). It is important to remember that when programmes were first introduced into British probation (see, for example, Raynor and Vanstone 1997; Vanstone 2000) they were intended as a supplement to 'normal' supervision or an enhancement of it, not as a substitute for it.

Concerning the second belief that 'there is a technical fix for everything', this shows itself mainly in an exaggerated optimism about information technology and other 'scientific' procedures, which on occasion has proved counterproductive. It is natural and appropriate that a newly unified Service will aspire to greater uniformity of practice through central control, and there is no shortage of examples from the past where a more consistent approach would have helped (see the discussion of 'myths of nostalgia' below). However, even Napoleon's insistence on common weights and measures throughout the Empire had to compromise with reality sometimes. Recent years have seen a number of examples of essential new procedures being hugely delayed by dependency on commissioned software which is never delivered on time or in full working order (a lesson which could surely have been learned from other government departments in advance). Case recording and management software (CRAMS) and 'interim' accredited programmes software (IAPS) have both experienced major problems and delays, interrupting the introduction of important practices such as monitoring the effectiveness of programmes, and sometimes forcing a resort to unsatisfactory interim paper versions.

Another example concerns the critical area of risk and need assessment. Throughout the 'what works' literature we learn that rehabilitative work with offenders is more likely to be effective if it is informed by assessments of risk and need (Andrews *et al.* 1990; Andrews and Bonta 1998; Roberts 1995). Development of assessment systems, therefore, needs to proceed in parallel with the development of programmes, or it is difficult to ensure that when programmes are 'rolled out' they will be made available to the people most likely to benefit. Probation services in Britain began to experiment with risk-need instruments in the mid-1990s, mostly the established Canadian LSI-R or the locally developed ACE system (see Roberts *et al.* 1996; Raynor *et al.* 2000). Both of these was evaluated and were clearly accurate and useful enough to improve practice where they were applied; by 1999 about half the Probation Service were using one or the other. At that point the Home Office decided to develop its own risk/need assessment instrument, announcing that it would be ready for introduction by August 2000 and therefore would save time compared to the previously announced tendering exercise (Robinson 2001).

This decision effectively blighted the development of ACE and LSI-R in England and Wales, since most probation areas preferred to wait for the Home Office product. Although the result, the Offender Assessment System (OASys), is an impressive instrument with excellent scientific support and validation through pilot studies, and will certainly have an impact on practice when its use becomes general, it is still in the process of being 'rolled out' and is not yet in general use at the time of writing. Moreover, it is fairly complex and was always intended to be used in an on-screen version, but has had to be introduced in a time-consuming paper version because the software is not yet available. The Prison Service will not use it until the software is available, so the benefits of uniformity across the penal system have yet to be delivered. Meanwhile the critical years for the introduction of evidence-based methods into probation areas have passed without the consistent use of any form of evidence-based risk/need assessment, although simple and feasible methods were available eight years ago. (Other jurisdictions which adopted good-enough methods in the 1990s have had a rather different experience: see, for example, Heath *et al.* 2002.) No doubt many lessons about implementation are being learned in what is, to be fair, still a fairly new national management structure.

Nostalgic illusions

The seventh and final source of misunderstanding which needs to be mentioned here is at least partly a myth of nostalgia, the belief that *everything was better in the old days*, when practitioner autonomy and 'established methods' (NAPO 2002) provided all the guarantees of effectiveness that were needed. I can certainly remember the attractions of the relative autonomy I experienced as a probation officer in the 1970s, though even then we complained about bureaucracy and interference, questioned whether senior probation officers were necessary, and grumbled about heavy caseloads and having to keep records up to date. Autonomy may allow good practice to flourish, but unfortunately it does exactly the same for bad practice. Joel Fischer (1976) used to argue that this was a major reason for the 'no significant benefit' findings of controlled studies of social work's effectiveness during the 1970s: the effects of the bad practice cancelled out the effects of the good, and researchers had not managed to distinguish between the two and assess their effects separately. It is also difficult to develop and build on good practice in an environment where each practitioner learns separately, and knowledge does not accumulate because there is no structured evaluation or organisational learning.

However, the strongest arguments against the 'autonomous practitioner' model rest on evaluation of its results. We are still waiting at the time of writing for definitive evaluation of the range of probation 'Pathfinder' programmes, but there is evidence from earlier British probation projects that well-designed programmes, implemented with integrity, can result in improvements in reconviction rates, particularly when compared with those achieved by similar offenders who receive custodial sentences (Raynor 1988; Roberts 1989; Raynor and Vanstone 1997). However, national comparisons of the reconviction rates of people supervised by probation officers, compared to those released from prison, consistently show little or no difference in outcome when differences in initial risk of reconviction are taken into account (for example, Lloyd *et al.* 1994; Kershaw *et al.* 1999; Prime 2002). The overall performance of the Service has not matched the achievements of some pioneering special projects. Similar problems have arisen when, instead of systematically following practices *designed* to be effective, officers have largely been left to provide whatever services they pleased.

One of the clearest examples of this was the IMPACT study (Folkard *et al.* 1976), which began the 'nothing works' era in British probation. This famous study allocated probationers at random to standard or 'intensive' caseloads to see if the results were better when probation officers had more time to work with offenders, but did not specify what the officers should do with the extra time. Instead they seem to have offered a mixture of more of what they would normally have done ('established methods') with a few innovations they would not normally have had time to try. The overall result was that the experimental (intensive caseload) group reconvicted slightly but not significantly more than the control (normal caseload) group. The only group which appeared to benefit from experimental status was a fairly small number of offenders who combined high self-assessed problems with low 'criminal tendencies', which suggests that a number of officers may have been using counselling-based methods which met some needs of this group, but not of other groups more typical of the offender population (Raynor 1978; Folkard 1981). Overall, getting more probation input was slightly less beneficial than getting less.

A more recent example of the results of local autonomy in the development and implementation of practice is Andrew Underdown's survey of 'effective practice' initiatives for the Probation Inspectorate (Underdown 1998), which paved the way for the introduction of much more central direction and leadership in the promotion of 'what works'. Briefly, the survey identified 267 projects and programmes which were claimed by local probation areas (then relatively autonomous rather than, as now, part of a national service) to be examples of the application of 'effective practice' principles. Out of these 267, even a relatively benign scrutiny could find only *four* which had been competently evaluated and showed some positive results (and this included one which had somehow been omitted from the responses to the original survey). Other researchers around the same time found that many probation areas which claimed to be running effective programmes were unable to say how many offenders had done them (Hedderman and Sugg 1997).

Other issues which should give rise to concern about the effects of local autonomy include the 'down tariff' drift of probation orders (now Community Rehabilitation Orders or CROs) to include more and more low-risk offenders. The proportion of probationers who are first offenders has been rising since 1991 (Raynor 1998) in spite of the 'risk principle' and long-established research evidence that first offenders on probation reconvict about twice as much as first offenders who are fined (Walker *et al.*

1981). This almost certainly reduces the overall effectiveness of probation/CROs. Wide variations in performance are also known to exist, both between officers (at least in Australia: see Trotter 2000) and between local probation areas now that these are being measured by audit and by national 'performance reports' (for example Wallis 2002). In general this seems to be a field where some external measurement of performance is important: as long ago as the 1960s, research on counselling and psychotherapy (Truax and Carkhuff 1967) was suggesting that while effective therapists are quite good at evaluating their own work, ineffective therapists consistently believe themselves to be more effective than they are. Moreover, they tend (if left to themselves) to become even less effective over time, but their belief in their own effectiveness becomes, according to Truax and Carkhuff, stronger rather than weaker.

More examples could be given, but this should be enough to indicate that the empirical support for practitioner autonomy is not strong. However, the desire to recreate the past is fuelled by the very real difficulties of the present: the rapid roll-out of new programmes and methods has coincided with major reorganisation to set up a national service; with new management and funding arrangements; new area boards replacing committees; and a redrawing of boundaries which has created newly amalgamated areas still struggling to bring different systems and structures together. Whether it was wise to try to tackle all these problems at the same time is a management question which lies outside the scope of this paper, though there are examples of services which have improved their effectiveness without such major restructuring (Heath *et al.* 2002). One particularly unnecessary touch, insisted on by politicians, was the decision to confuse practitioners, sentencers and the public by changing the familiar names of Probation and Community Service Orders to Community Rehabilitation Orders and Community Punishment Orders, when some continuity in a period of major change might have been more helpful.

The current period of transition in probation services is full of stresses and paradoxes: as I write, probation officers are embarking on national industrial action over workloads, while the Home Office has just published evidence that both probation and prisons are on course to meet the ambitious crime-reduction targets agreed with the Treasury (Prime 2002).

Many observers are impressed by the knowledge and enthusiasm about 'what works' to be found among staff who are trained to deliver and manage new programmes, while some other staff become stressed and disaffected and key tasks like case management or preparing court reports can suffer as a consequence. This echoes the findings of earlier research (Raynor and Vanstone 1997) that greater enthusiasm and optimism about programmes were to be found among those who actually delivered them. But in a service like probation, where different activities reinforce and depend on each other, such uneven development is clearly undesirable and needs to be addressed, which in turn requires time and resources. It is also important to recognise that not all the strains and difficulties are consequences of evidence-based practice. Often, as in the example of name-changes, they are quite the reverse.

In short, the way forward for probation services seems more likely to be found by broadening and extending the evidence-based approach than by abandoning it. If the National Probation Service wants to pursue the reforming mission shared by most of its staff, by providing alternatives to more punitive and less constructive sentences, it is not enough to show that an ever-increasing prison population is not cost-effective. It is also necessary to *demonstrate* (not simply to claim) that community penalties can provide greater tangible public benefit through more reparation to the community, greater opportunities for offenders to change their behaviour, and in the long run a reduction in offending. Evidence-based practice offers a better chance of demonstrating this because it creates opportunities for more effective delivery and more systematic accumulation of knowledge about what works and what doesn't. It does not, of course, guarantee success, but neither does anything else: the whole probation enterprise remains politically vulnerable to populist 'tough on crime' policies. However, collecting and communicating the evidence of effectiveness is itself part of the political campaign to defend reason and humanity in criminal justice. It would be the height of irresponsibility to neglect what is now a serious body of accumulated knowledge in favour of a preference for not knowing.

References

Andrews, D.A. and Bonta, J. (1995) *The Level of Service Inventory – Revised: Manual.* Toronto: Multi-Health Systems Inc.

Andrews, D.A. and Bonta, J. (1998) *The Psychology of Criminal Conduct.* Cincinnati: Anderson.

Andrews, D.A., Zinger, I., Hoge, R.D., Bonta, J., Gendreau, P. and Cullen, F.T. (1990) 'Does correctional treatment work? A clinically relevant and psychologically informed meta-analysis.' *Criminology 28*, 369–404.

Bottoms, A.E. and McWilliams, W. (1979) 'A non-treatment paradigm for probation practice.' *British Journal of Social Work 9*, 159–202.

Brody, S.R. (1976) *The Effectiveness of Sentencing.* London: HMSO.

Clark, D. and Howden-Windell, J. (2000) *A Retrospective Study of Criminogenic Factors in the Female Prison Population.* Report to the Home Office, unpublished.

Davies, M. (2002) *The Blackwell Companion to Social Work.* Oxford: Blackwell.

Dowden, C. and Andrews, D. (1999) 'What works for female offenders: A meta-analytic review.' *Crime and Delinquency 45*, 4, 438–452.

Farrington, D. (2002) 'Developmental criminology and risk-focused prevention.' In M. Maguire, R. Morgan and R. Reiner (eds) *The Oxford Handbook of Criminology.* Oxford: Oxford University Press.

Fischer, J. (1976) *The Effectiveness of Social Casework.* Springfield: C.C. Thomas.

Folkard, M.S., Smith, D.E. and Smith, D.D. (1976) *IMPACT. Intensive Matched Probation and After-Care Treatment. Volume II. The Results of the Experiment* (Home Office Research Study 36). London: HMSO.

Folkard, S. (1981) 'Second thoughts on IMPACT.' In E.M. Goldberg and N. Connelly (eds) *Evaluative Research in Social Care.* London: Heinemann.

Foren, R. and Bailey, R. (1968) *Authority in Social Casework.* Oxford: Pergamon Press.

Gelsthorpe, L. (2001) 'Accountability: Difference and diversity in the delivery of community penalties.' In A.E. Bottoms, L. Gelsthorpe and S. Rex (eds) *Community Penalties: Change and Challenges.* Cullompton: Willan.

Gorman, K. (2001) 'Cognitive behaviourism and the Holy Grail.' *Probation Journal 48*, 1, 3–9.

Harris, R. (1989) 'Social work in society or punishment in the community?' In R. Shaw and K. Haines (eds) *The Criminal Justice System: A Central Role for the Probation Service.* Cambridge: Institute of Criminology.

Heath, B., Raynor, P. and Miles, H. (2002) 'What Works in Jersey: The first ten Years.' *VISTA 7*, 3, 202–208.

Hedderman, C. and Sugg, D. (1997) *The Influence of Cognitive Approaches, With a Survey of Probation Programmes* (Home Office Research Study 171, Part 2). London: Home Office.

Her Majesty's Inspectorate of Probation (2002) *Annual Report 2001–2002.* London: Home Office.

Hollis, F. (1964) *Casework: A Psychosocial Therapy.* New York: Random House.

Home Office (1984) *Probation Service in England and Wales: Statement of National Objectives and Priorities.* London: Home Office.

Hudson, B. (2002) 'Gender issues in penal policy and penal theory.' In P. Carlen (ed.) *Women and Punishment.* Cullompton: Willan.

Kendall, K. (2002) 'Time to think again about cognitive-behavioural programmes.' In P. Carlen (ed.) *Women and Punishment.* Cullompton: Willan.

Kershaw, C., Goodman, J. and White, S. (1999) *Reconvictions of Offenders Sentenced or Discharged from Prison in 1995, England and Wales* (Statistical Bulletin 19/99). London: Home Office.

Lewis, S., Vennard, J., Maguire, M., Raynor, P., Vanstone, M., Raybould, S. and Rix, J. (2002) *The Resettlement of Short-Term Prisoners: An Evaluation of Seven Pathfinders.* Report to the Research, Development and Statistics Directorate, Home Office.

Lipsey, M. (1992) 'Juvenile delinquency treatment: A meta-analytic enquiry into the variability of effects.' In T. Cook, H. Cooper, D.S. Cordray, H. Hartmann, L.V. Hedges, R.L. Light, T.A. Louis and F. Mosteller (eds) *Meta-Analysis for Explanation: A Case-book.* New York: Russell Sage.

Lipton, D., Martinson, R. and Wilks, J. (1975) *The Effectiveness of Correctional Treatment.* New York: Praeger.

Lloyd, C., Mair, G. and Hough, M. (1994) *Explaining Reconviction Rates: A Critical Analysis.* London: HMSO.

McGuire, J. (ed.) (1995) *What Works: Reducing Reoffending.* Chichester: Wiley.

McGuire, J. and Priestley, P. (1985) *Offending Behaviour: Skills and Stratagems for Going Straight.* London: Batsford.

McIvor, G. (1990) *Sanctions for Serious or Persistent Offenders.* Stirling: Social Work Research Centre.

Mair, G. (2000) 'Credible accreditation?' *Probation Journal 47*, 4, 268–271.

Merrington, S. and Stanley, S. (2000) 'Doubts about the What Works Initiative.' *Probation Journal 47*, 272–275.

Meyer, H.J., Borgatta, E.F. and Jones, W.C. (1965) *Girls at Vocational High.* New York: Russell Sage.

National Association of Probation Officers (2002) *Accredited Programmes Policy.* London: NAPO.

OASys Development Team (2001) *The Offender Assessment System (OASys).* London: Home Office.

Perry, D. (2002) 'Racially motivated offenders: The way forward.' *Probation Journal 49*, 4, 305–309.

Powers, E. and Witmer, J. (1951) *An Experiment in the Treatment of Delinquency.* New York: Columbia University Press.

Powis, B. and Walmsley, R. (2002) *Programmes for Black and Asian Offenders on Probation: Lessons for Developing Practice* (Home Office Research Study 250). London: Home Office.

Prime, J. (2002) *Progress Made Against Home Office Public Service Agreement Target 10,* Online Report 16/02. London: Home Office. www.homeoffice.gov.uk/rds/pdfs2/redsolr1602.pdf.

Raynor, P. (1978) 'Compulsory persuasion: a problem for correctional social work.' *British Journal of Social Work 8*, 4, 411–424.

Raynor, P. (1985) *Social Work, Justice and Control*. Oxford: Blackwell.

Raynor, P. (1988) *Probation as an Alternative to Custody*. Aldershot: Avebury.

Raynor, P. (1998) 'Reading probation statistics: A critical comment.' *VISTA 3*, 181–185.

Raynor, P. and Vanstone, M. (1996) 'Reasoning and rehabilitation in Britain: The results of the Straight Thinking On Probation (STOP) programme.' *International Journal of Offender Therapy and Comparative Criminology 40*, 272–284.

Raynor, P. and Vanstone, M. (1997) *Straight Thinking On Probation (STOP): The Mid Glamorgan Experiment* (Probation Studies Unit Report 4). Oxford: Centre for Criminological Research.

Raynor, P. and Vanstone, M. (2002) *Understanding Community Penalties*. Buckingham: Open University Press.

Raynor, P., Kynch, J., Roberts, C. and Merrington, M. (2000) *Risk and Need Assessment in Probation Services: An Evaluation* (Home Office Research Study 211). London: Home Office.

Roberts, C. (1989) *Hereford and Worcester Probation Service Young Offender Project: First Evaluation Report*. Oxford: Department of Social and Administrative Studies.

Roberts, C. (1995) 'Effective practice and service delivery.' In J. McGuire (ed.) *What Works: Reducing Reoffending*. Chichester: Wiley.

Roberts, C., Burnett, R., Kirby, A. and Hamill, H. (1996) *A System for Evaluating Probation Practice* (Probation Studies Unit Report 1). Oxford: Centre for Criminological Research.

Robinson, G. (2001) 'Power, knowledge and What Works in probation.' *Howard Journal of Criminal Justice 40*, 235–254.

Ross, R.R. and Fabiano, E.A. (1985) *Time to Think: A Cognitive Model of Delinquency Prevention and Offender Rehabilitation*. Johnson City, TN: Institute of Social Sciences and Arts.

Shaw, M. and Hannah-Moffatt, K. (2000) 'Gender, diversity and risk assessment in Canadian corrections.' *Probation Journal 47*, 3, 163–172.

Thorpe, D.H., Smith, D., Green, C.J. and Paley, J. (1980) *Out of Care*. London: Allen and Unwin.

Trotter, C. (2000) 'Social work education, pro-social modelling and effective probation practice.' *Probation Journal 47*, 256–261.

Truax, C. and Carkhuff, R. (1967) *Towards Effective Counselling and Psychotherapy*. Chicago: Aldine.

Underdown, A. (1998) *Strategies for Effective Offender Supervision: Report of the HMIP What Works Project*. London: Home Office.

Vanstone, M. (2000) 'Cognitive-behavioural work with offenders in the UK: A history of influential endeavour.' *Howard Journal of Criminal Justice 39*, 2, 171–183.

Walker, N., Farrington, D. and Tucker, G. (1981) 'Reconviction rates of adult males after different sentences.' *British Journal of Criminology 21*, 357–360.

Wallis, E. (2002) *National Probation Service Performance Report 6*. London: National Probation Directorate.

The Contributors

Jan Fook is Director of the Centre for Professional Development at La Trobe University, Melbourne. She has taught social work and welfare for over 20 years in several Australian universities. Her interests are in critical practice and the nature of professional expertise. Her most recent book is *Social Work: Critical Theory and Practice* (2002).

Paul Keeling is Research Manager at the Lifeline Project in Manchester. He is responsible for maintaining Lifeline's long-established tradition of high-quality applied research in the field of problematic drug use and service development.

Karen Kibblewhite is Senior Researcher at the Lifeline Project. She is involved in needs assessment, service mapping and service development strategies.

Colin Pritchard is Research Professor of Psychiatric Social Work at Bournemouth University, having returned to work after retirement from the University of Southampton, where he held a Chair in the Mental Health Group of the Faculty of Medicine, Health and Biological Sciences. His most recent research has been on child abuse, truancy and school exclusion, and suicide.

Peter Raynor holds a personal Chair in Applied Social Studies at the University of Wales, Swansea, working in the School of Social Science and International Development and the Centre for Criminal Justice and Criminology. He is a member of the Home Office's Joint Prisons and Probation Programme Accreditation Panel. His most recent book is *Understanding Community Penalties* (2002, with Maurice Vanstone).

Bob Sapey has been Lecturer in Social Work at Lancaster University since 1999. His main research interests are disability and technology, especially as they relate to social work practice. With colleagues at Lancaster, he is currently researching the social implications of increased wheelchair use.

David Smith is Professor of Criminology in the Department of Applied Social Science, Lancaster University. A former probation officer, he held social work posts at Lancaster from 1976 to 2002. He has researched and published widely on probation and youth justice policy and practice, and more recently on racist violence.

Zoë Smith is a researcher with the Lifeline Project in Manchester. She works with problem drug users in the north of England on the assessment of service need.

Claire Taylor is a Research Associate at the University of Nottingham, working jointly in the Centre for Social Work and the School of Law. She obtained her PhD at Lancaster University. She is co-author with Moira Peelo and Keith Soothill of *Making Sense of Criminology* (2002).

Julie Taylor-Browne is the Director of Kanzeon Consulting, a specialist consultancy in sexual violence and child abuse. She is a former researcher for the Home Office, and an Honorary Fellow of the Department of Applied Social Science, Lancaster University.

Subject Index

Author Index